SELF-H...

ITS THEORY, TECHNIQUE
AND APPLICATION

by MELVIN POWERS

Author

Self-Hypnosis
Dynamic Thinking
A Practical Guide to Self-Hypnosis
Advanced Techniques of Hypnosis
Mental-Power Through Sleep-Suggestion
A Practical Guide to Better Concentration

Foreword by Dr. Jean Bordeaux

Published by
Melvin Powers

WILSHIRE BOOK COMPANY
12015 Sherman Road
No. Hollywood, California 91605
Telephone: (213) 875-1711

Printed by

HAL LEIGHTON PRINTING COMPANY
P.O. Box 3952
North Hollywood, California 91605
Telephone: (213) 983-1105

Printed in the United States of America

Library of Congress Catalog Card Number: 55-11981

ISBN 0-87980-138-7

CONTENTS

CONTENTS

FOREWORD

There are innumerable books on the general subject of hypnosis, but only a few on self-hypnosis. Here is a book which shows the increasing importance of the subject in our modern world. The average person who feels he has failed to show to the world his full potentialities of personality and success starts trotting from one therapist or counselor to another, endeavoring by unending series of interviews with them to attain the sought-for success.

The fact is that "God helps those who help themselves." One of the finest ways to self improvement is through judicious use of self-hypnosis. All present day advertising and propaganda are based on the use of suggestion which is the foundation stone of self-hypnosis. As the author explains, we think with the conscious part of the mind. He sets forth five cogent reasons for his belief that each of us does have a subconscious area somewhere within us, and that as we motivate our actions therefrom, we begin to achieve.

Along with a brief explanation of dreams, concrete examples are given of subconscious motivation to illustrate the relationships and the tie-ins between that area and the conscious mind. Ten beneficial steps are carefully explained and by following these, the reader can help himself through self-analysis.

Various schools of psychotherapy are discussed and six specific cases ranging from mild to extremely serious emotional upsets are specifically described. There is a great need for psychotherapy and this book seeks to meet that need.

"What is hypnosis?" is a question frequently asked. Its wide range of startling phenomena is set forth herein and analyzed in such a way as to permit the author to state his theory of hypnotism which is novel and yet sensible. He also gives a helpful explanation of how we learn new habits. The actual techniques of self-hypnosis are fully explained. When properly used, these can open up a new way of life for any ambitious, persistent individual.

Jean Bordeaux, Ph.D.

PREFACE

Thomas Henry Huxley, renowned British biologist and writer, in speaking of the nature of man remarked brilliantly that, "The rung of a ladder was never meant to rest upon, but only to hold a man's foot long enough to enable him to put the other somewhat higher." That statement illustrated the nature of man more simply and clearly than many a volume I have read on the subject of man's purposes and his destiny.

Man, that strange, wonderful creature; made in the image of God; endowed with both mind and a soul; "The paragon of animals," in the words of Shakespeare; this restless searcher after truths; undaunted climber of mountains; this human creature that plumbs the mysteries of the seas and brings up its precious treasures for use and scientific investigation; this man who has created and destroyed mighty civilizations in the past and who has in recent years found the secret of the atom; this man who seems capable of knowing and achieving all things on this planet has yet been unable to achieve the most important insight of all — adequate knowledge of himself.

This volume is concerned with man and his relationship to the society in which he lives. It is not the purpose of this book to make the insight seem simple and easy to come by. That would be a deception, since man is actually a complex and subtle being composed of both a biological and social nature which both come into play in his every day life.

Thomas Huxley's "man on the ladder" mentioned previously is a restless climber and searcher, indeed, but wouldn't man be much better off if he learned more about his own essential nature first before devoting so much time and energy to uncovering the mysteries of the universe? T h e s e are exciting and important, of course, but certainly not more so than man's knowledge of himself, his resources and his development.

To this end, I have written this book titled, "Self-Hypnosis, Its Theory, Technique and Application." It is one that will require careful reading and study. It is written primarily for the advanced student of hypnosis with the hope that it will lead him to still greater heights in his personal development. It is hoped that the book will also serve as a stepping-stone in awakening a keen interest in many related subjects.

Ever since Plato divided the faculties of the human mind into feeling, willing and thinking — a profoundly influential theory — psychologists have tended to explain all thoughts and actions along these lines.

To feeling — so they have said — corresponds our faculty of *sympathy*. To willing, they liken *imitation;* and to thinking, *suggestion.*

These have been called "The Big Three" in the history of social psychology, of which "suggestion is the most important."*

But even though it be true that suggestion, more than any other "simple and sovereign theory," has been preferred *by technical thinkers* as an explanation of basic

*Ref.: "Handbook Of Social Psychology," p. 24 in the lead article, "The Historical Background Of Modern Social Psychology," 1954, by Professor Gordon W. Allport, Harvard University.

human actions, how can *we* here and now grasp its importance?

It is the purpose of this book to convince the reader that suggestion is of vital importance for him. Also, everything in the following pages will have a direct bearing on his personal happiness. Furthermore, by revealing many of the techniques of *self-hypnosis,* we are going to open the road that leads, *through suggestion,* to the self-realization, success and personal satisfaction, that the reader wants. This is why he is reading this book, which we have tried to load with dynamite for him. With it, if he will be patient, we shall try to sweep away restraining obstacles (negative ideas) from his path.

And, to continue our figure of speech, we can do two more things. First, we can furnish "field glasses" which will show him something of what he may make of himself. It will be "the city on the hill" that he sees shining far above him — but not too far above. And second, we shall set down, in plain words, techniques for self-realization — for the using, *through* self-hypnosis, of the exciting, world-important *power of suggestion.*

Melvin Powers

**12015 Sherman Road,
No. Hollywood, California 91605**

CHAPTER I

Suggestion and Its Application

In this chapter we want to do three things. First it is important that we grasp the essential meaning of the term suggestion. Second, we wish to see how it reveals itself in all the phenomena of society. Third, in order to use it ourselves, we must know how it has already been used, in history and in the writings of great social thinkers. Unless we have this background, we shall not be able to apply, for our own benefit, the force in question.

Suggestion is defined as "1. the inducing, or the attempt at inducing of an idea, belief, decision, action, etc., by one individual in another through stimulation, whether verbal or otherwise, but exclusive of argument; 2. the stimulus, usually verbal in nature, by which one individual seeks to arouse action in another by circumventing the critical, integrative functions." (Dictionary Of Psychology Howard C. Warren, ed., p. 267).

The above phrase "exclusive of argument" shows us that suggestion lies in an *uncritical acceptance* of beliefs. These do not always come from others. They can, and often are, given to a person by himself!

Also, they are "self-given" in at least two different ways. The suggestions may flow either from the conscious self to the subconscious self . . . or it may be a suggestion arising from the subconsciousness . . . and dictating to the consciousness. Clearly the task of explaining the phenomena of suggestion and hypnosis is going to be a doubly difficult one.

The thoughtful reader may well be wondering what the value of suggestion is, since it is defined as *uncritical* acceptance of beliefs. The answer to this is an eye-opener, for it tends to make us all social-minded at once. It is, that each of us, as an individual, has neither the time, the opportunity nor the ability to *test all things*. And, therefore, we must accept almost all of them as untested, that is, through faith and the rapid medium of suggestion. Otherwise, we would not be able to use what civilization has already forged out for us. We can't reason out and prove every statement before we believe it, otherwise we would never find time to grow civilized at all.

To grasp what suggestion is, means that we realize what an overwhelming proportion of our experience it accounts for. What could be more important, therefore, than to begin to understand this faculty for itself?

And so we come to our second point: how does suggestion reveal itself? That is, in how many facets of social living can we see suggestion working powerfully, on billions of people, year after year, for better or for worse?

Here again, from another angle, we see its staggering extent. Since most *belief* has come to us via suggestion, we see that *faith,* religious or otherwise, was born of suggestion.

Propaganda . . . "organized publicity used as a means of influencing attitudes" . . . is suggestion, seen in a hundred different modern fields including all of advertising and much of business and politics, from the tinkle of the "Good Humor Man's" chimes to the deadly-earnest of the "cold war."

Organizations, especially the thousands of different spontaneous kinds which flourish in a democracy, from Girl Scouts through fraternal orders, etc. to huge trade associations and unions, all stand for something. They must not only keep their own memberships *sold* on the various things they stand for, but, if they want new members and a favorable public opinion, they must, through suggestion, sell the public on their merits.

Art in all its forms depends clearly on the artist *getting through* to the public whatever feelings, impressions or messages he wants to convey. An art form such as painting on canvas or a novel is simply a favorite mode of suggestion chosen by the artist to influence a public.

We may instance this — and deepen our appreciation of suggestion as a techique of communication between minds — by music therapy. This rapidly growing field, to which young pioneers like Earl W. Brabandt, Jr. are devoting their lives, is based on *subtlety* of suggestion, especially when it is musical. Let us see *how* suggestion is subtle, so that we can appreciate its power. Both speech and music are apprehended by us through the sense of hearing: and both can influence also our centers for emotional feeling, notably the thalamus and hypothalamus. But speech *can* be ignored, not heard or attended to, with relative ease by a patient who is mentally disturbed or partially unconscious; whereas music "steals into our senses, ere we are aware." It influences our emotions and — whether we are willing to *think* about things or not — changes our moods. In the use of music therapy, therefore, the strategy is to *key* the music at first to the original mood of the patient, then to change the type of music in the direction desired. And so, a person who cannot even be "reached" verbally, can be won back to health *musically*.

Also, in observing the truly awe-inspiring significance of suggestion in human affairs, we must admit that both *temperament* and *character* are largely matters of suggestion. Here, the suggestion tends to be *inherited* and/or *constant*. For example, an active or a cheerful temperament represents underlying motor tendencies to act or to feel in certain ways: and a person's character consists of ingrained attitudes and beliefs which tend to stay with him through thick and thin. Much of the entire personality consists of these perennial *streams of suggestion* which proceed through one for better or for worse.

That these streams of suggestion can be *changed* to our betterment is the great insight of today.

But what about *national* character and temperament? Surely this is not a matter of suggestion too! Surely this has no connection with man's will, being but stubborn facts of nature. There is no space to go into this fascinating field, but modern anthropologists tell us (as David Hume did long ago in his brilliant essay on "National Character"), that the latter is rather an effect of the "cultural climate" than of heredity. We must all have noticed that individuals of different racial strains, brought here at a tender age and raised in our culture, are surprisingly American in actions and outlook. All around them, as they grew up, suggestion played its powerful part; and they absorbed mannerisms, beliefs and practices as a sponge does water.

For example, *sisu,* defined as "indomitable, high-hearted courage that carries one beyond natural capacity," and other qualities such as "deep feeling for nature and art," is said to be the Finnish national character. An article in the June, 1955 Readers Digest says the *sisu* qualities exist in every Finn, as the building blocks of basic character. These are all *in* their culture, taught to the growing child over his formative years by nothing but suggestion, "exclusive of argument." And there are scores of similar studies dealing with other sets of national characteristics.

While noting now the vast fields over which the power of suggestion extends, we must recall that *its power over the person* and *his personal power over it* are really our subjects. And that, just as poor reactions such as failure, frustration and unhappiness are all too often due to *unfortunate* self-suggestions, so, just as truly, are outstanding success and vibrant happiness due to the correct,

[15]

scientific, and well-informed suggestions such as you will find in this book.

But first we must answer the third question set for ourselves in this chapter. Namely, what has been the fate, so far in man's thought, of this great concept of suggestion? It was identified in 1866 by the French scientist Liebeault with *hypnotism*: mild suggestibility meant a very light hypnotic mood.

Bernheim, head of the Nancy school of psychiatry, stated, in basic agreement, in 1884, that suggestion is a natural and normal "ideo-motor" process, which can result in hypnotism. By ideo-motor he meant that a firmly planted *idea* of movement can result in the actual movement which is its object.

But the "villain" in the piece now appeared. He was Jean Martin Charcot, head of the Salpetriere school of psychiatry in Paris, who maintained, using melodramatic demonstrations, that only the hysteroid type of personality could be hypnotized.

This is definitely not so, and has been disproved thousands of times by now. But though two of Charcot's students, Pierre Janet and Boris Sidis, toned their master's position down greatly, a book was written by another of Charcot's disciples which distorted the entire subject of suggestion.

This was Gustave Le Bon's "The Crowd," (1895), perhaps the most influential book on social psychology ever written, despite its falsifications. Le Bon, with the murderous mobs of the French Revolution in mind, said that the leading characteristic of "crowds" was a suggestibility in which normal intelligence is overshadowed by animal instincts. Thus a crowd always has a collective mind inferior to the individual minds in it. And though many of his observations on the lynch type of mob were shrewd and true, "His treatment was dogmatic and biased and was colored by an aristocratic fear of a new era of crowds and an age of socialism." (Social Psychology," by S. Stansfeld Sargent, p. 11).

Stevenson's "Strange Case Of Dr. Jekyll And Mr. Hyde" (1886) seemed to confirm the general impression that there is a relatively "animal" side to each of us which is highly amenable to irrational suggestion, but which is unfortunately a trouble-maker.

Social scientists pounced on this doctrine of the dual nature of man, one side of which could be dissociated and bestialized. For it *gave them a theory* to explain the worst forms of crowd phenomena, such as mass hysteria, irrational crazes and booms, social leadership by demagogues and charlatans who arouse the worst in us, etc.

Another pupil of Charcot's, namely Morton Prince, renamed his "Journal Of Abnormal Psychology" the "Journal Of Abnormal And Social Psychology," thus assuming, as is done to this day, that social suggestion is a blood relative of social abnormality.

Many writers have followed this original trend, either holding, with Charcot that suggestion is the royal road to personality disintegration, or that it can be relied on, as a social force, to arouse the worst in human nature.

What is the *truth* about suggestion and its possible end-product, hypnosis? All are agreed that suggestion is a tremendous force. What then is its actual nature?

The truth about this force is that, like thousands of other instrumentalities whether material or mental, it is in itself *neither good nor bad*. Everything depends on how it is used. The power of suggestibility in man is an accomplished actor which can star in the highest roles if given the chance. This is what we are asking the reader to do, and will show him how.

The unfortunate Charcotian emphasis on suggestion and hypnotism has thus had a double influence, namely on clinical psychology and on social psychology. In the former case, viewing the individual alone, organic evolution has taught us that a person represents a complicated unit of some *five* different brain units, rather than one: and that suggestion can, and usually does, help him to *keep* these units associated and working smoothly together, rather than to dissociate them and rob the brain-owner of his psychic strength.

As for the social situation, it is not suggestion as such that causes riots, mob scenes, wars, etc., but *surplus energy,* which spills over from time to time and causes events which most people deplore. The forces of *right conduct* are *suggested* to us as truly as ever its opposite was, and more successfully as time goes on. In other words, *mass sentiments can be good ones,* and what each of us owes to education and to the culture which has given us all we have by way of civilization and knowledge, is greater than he can ever pay.

We have seen that suggestion is a powerful force — perhaps the strongest of all social influences — which got off to a bad start historically, by being associated in men's minds with destructiveness and irrationality. This naturally has made it very difficult for people to use the force rightly. First they must recognize it for what it is, then they must know the basic ideas and the techniques needed to build with it.

To this end we should see how the mind operates, in its two widely recognized phases of *conscious* and *subconscious.* We must realize how suggestion operates throughout this life of the mind. Let us turn first to the former phase.

CHAPTER II

The Conscious Mind

This is one of the most difficult of all subjects to analyze, and for two reasons. First, the *contents* of the conscious mind are certainly part of the problem of analysis; yet since these include what life itself means to us, we must apparently analyze *everything* of which we can be aware. What an order!

Second, consciousness itself (not its contents) is a kind of lightning-like activity, highly volatile, rapidly changing, elusive in the extreme. And we must realize that to some extent the task of analysis is impossible, since it is *with* consciousness that we must *study* consciousness. That is, consciousness is itself a *presupposition* about any thinking we do about it. Have you ever seen a dog chase his tail, and catch it? But we shall try: — for the subject is of vital importance to us.

Fortunately, William James' famous description of "The Stream Of Thought" can help us. (ch. 9 in his "Principles Of Psychology"). We shall quote his five points directly. He says:

"1. Every thought tends to be part of a personal consciousness.

"2. Within each personal consciousness, thought is always changing.

"3. Within each personal consciousness, thought is sensibly continuous.

"4. It always appears to deal with objects independent of itself.

"5. It is interested in some parts of these objects to the exclusion of others, and welcomes or rejects — *chooses* from among them, in a word — all the while."

And now to comment briefly on each of these points:

1. This means simply that your thoughts and feelings come to you as belonging peculiarly and uniquely to *you;* mine to me, etc. They are *special* for each person. It is true that sometimes thoughts can just *be,* apparently, as when a person is ill or mentally subnormal, lacks his usual self-integration, and doesn't realize that *he* is having the thought. But these times are rare: even when one "comes to" in a hospital, after a lapse of consciousness, the stock question is "Where am I?", not "Who am I?". Thoughts tend to be personal; a person knows his thoughts *are* his.

2. Mental processes are like quicksilver; they elude us even as we try, for purposes of analysis, to grasp them. Heraclitus, an early Greek philosopher, said that you can't step into the same river twice because, the second time you do, it isn't the same river. It is also just as true that *you* aren't the same you, on any second occasion.

Let us take but one example of these rapid changes

in us. The red cells in our blood-stream live from ten to thirty days. One-tenth to one-thirtieth of them are thus destroyed daily, and replacements must be created by bodily processes. "This would mean, on the basis of a ten-day age limit, the destruction and formation of 21,-000,000,000 (twenty-one billion) cells per minute." ("The Human Body And How It Works," p. 23, by Dr. Elbert Tokay, Permabooks, 1949).

Each of us is not a concrete substance but a *pattern* that continues in operation over the years! What is the *best* pattern for each of us; and how can we realize, strengthen and retain this best pattern? That is the question this book wants to help solve.

3. This point means that our minds tend to fill in, as long as we are alive and healthy, the *time-gaps* that exist between our various trains of thought. Sleep contributes most of these time-gaps, but as James says; "When Paul and Peter wake up in the same bed, and recognize that they have been asleep, each one of them mentally reaches back and makes connection with but *one* of the two streams of thought which were broken by sleeping hours; — so Peter's present instantly finds out Peter's past, and never by mistake knits itself on to that of Paul." (ibid., p. 238).

Also, these hookings-on of a person's past mental life with that of his present life are never too abrupt. Our various stages of thinking and feelings, of moods and ideas, tend to flow smoothly into one another. We have a certain definite sense of continuity, even after "a good night's sleep," — or perhaps because of it.

This "wonderful stream of our consciousness" does indeed, however, have a different pace to its parts. "Like a bird's life, it seems to be made of an alternation of flights and perchings." (ibid., p. 243). James means that some parts of our mental life, the "perchings," are more definite than other parts (vague tendencies, "unnamed states," etc.).

4. Always, so long as we are in a state of "normal" mental health, we feel strongly that we are in a *r e a l* world, and that the objects of our environment are *independent* of us. Anyone who thinks differently may be seriously bumped! One of the things the baby must learn is precisely this fact, that he is in a real world, and must be careful how he moves around in it.

In a larger sense, part of our problem is to realize what things are the most real, in the sense of being the most worthwhile.

5. And this brings us to James' last point, that the mind realizes relative worth by *choosing* certain objects and *modes of action,* and rejecting others. This causes the formation of *habits,* which is highly advisable when done through the use of *judgment, right suggestion,* and *will power.* One of the most important aspects of our conscious selves is the dynamic, effortful, striving part of us. We can change our natures: we are going to be striving for various things all our lives — even "peace and quiet" are objects of desire. We want therefore to

be sure we are expending our will power and energy toward the most valuable goals possible.

There are at least three other general characteristics of consciousness.

1. It has a structural relationship to the flow of time — that is, to the past, the present, and the future. To the past correspond our memories, to the present our *perceptions* (as of colors, moving shapes, etc.), and to the future our *purposes*.

2. Consciousness has different *levels*. Many great psychologists have noticed that consciousness is not a simple, one-level affair, but seems to come to us, as it were, in various depths. Indeed, the three recent leaders in this field, Sigmund Freud (1856-1939), Alfred Adler (1870-1937), Carl G. Jung (1875-1961) — and their disciples — are known as "depth psychologists."

To put it as briefly as possible, they have stressed these interesting facts about consciousness: a. its processes are the outcome of unsuspected *forces*, and so are never just superficial and accidental. b. these forces are frequently if not usually *unconscious*, a point upon which we shall dwell in the next chapter; c. the history of the childhood development of the individual should be known, in order to understand these forces and the resultant processes — this being of course the usual method of "psychoanalysis;" d. the levels may be three in number, the "conscious," the "preconscious" and the "unconscious." (There is another triple division in depth psychology, any one individual being regarded as a more or less successful synthesis of his "id," his "ego" and his "super-ego.")

We may well suspect from this that the human personality does indeed have great "depth," or various depths. Hypnotism confirms this. The extent to which a person can work beneficially with the various depths of his own personality, is the subject of this book.

The recognition of levels in consciousness is by no means limited to exponents of psychoanalysis. K. Westphal wrote about it in 1911, F. Seifert in 1917, and many others. A great European psychiatrist says, "The multitude of half-conscious actions cannot be over-estimated. A spark lights up in the peripheral visual field, (e.g.), and is received on a low level of intelligence; the eyes turn toward it, but since the spark is not worth sustained attention if they turn back to the object previously fixated — and this repeats itself thousands of times daily. — All these are will-actions of a low level of consciousness." (from "Medical Psychology," p. 105, by Paul Schilder, International Universities Press, 1953).

3. Consciousness is at any time, and therefore at all times, a *structuralized field* which shows continually changing degrees of clarity within its parts. William James has much to say, it is true, about our vague "fringe of consciousness" as against its clearer focal center. But to understand "the conscious mind" we need to appreciate further how complicated even this one point of *clarity* is.

[25]

There are, a. physical, b. physiological, and c. intellectual considerations here.

a. The *physical* conditions of the field of consciousness, and the clarity of its content, refer to the fact that externally originating *stimuli* (*outside* influences like light waves, temperature conditions, etc.) must at least be *available*, and must at least be *strong* enough, *near* enough, etc., to make us notice them. For example, the human animal won't perceive a red color unless light waves from that frequency band actually strike his optic apparatus.

b. The *physiological* conditions of the field of consciousness refer to the fact that our receiving apparatus for impressions — our eyes, ears, taste buds, etc., must be both *specific* and *sensitive*. *Specific* simply means that each sense organ must be of a definite enough nature to give us a clear-cut, recognizable impression. Thus a color, a taste, etc., must not be so unclear that it cannot form its own quality and become a definite part of our consciousness. *Sensitive* means that the sense organ itself must be in good enough working shape to *convey* the stimulus to the mind, for interpretation.

Not all of these stimuli have to come from outside of our bodies, otherwise we could not know what the conditions and states of affairs were *within* ourselves. We have hunger pangs, muscular sensations, etc. These are all messages *to* our minds from the various parts of our own bodies.

c. The more purely *intellectual* conditions of the field

of consciousness include *attention* and *set* or *attitude*. Attention refers to the fact that we usually *turn to* certain features in our field of consciousness, in order to see them more clearly, or concentrate on them. These features then occupy the center of our attention. For example, in seeing, we usually look directly at the object most interesting to us, which then, anatomically, occupies the very center of the visual field in each eye, a place of clearest vision on each retina called the fovea.

As regards *set,* or the more general term *attitude,* this means that we can not only arrange our entire bodies and minds, as it were, in *anticipation* of a certain experience, so that we can give it our best and fullest attention when it happens to us; but also means that what we *tend* to set ourselves for, and to notice, is dependent in surprising degree upon what our *past experience* has trained us to notice and to think of as valuable.

The thoughtful reader will see that, so far, we have mentioned only a few of the general *characteristics* of consciousness. Two further questions must now be asked: namely, what are the actual *contents* of consciousness; and what are the *mechanisms* which make consciousness possible?

But first, let us clear up one important matter — the relationship between *consciousness* and *mind.* The writer's suggestion is to conceive mind in *one* or *both* of the following ways: —

1. By a person's "mind" is meant simply the sum-

total of all his states of consciousness and experiences from the beginning of his conscious life to the end of it. If his conscious life began *before* he was actually born — as it probably did — include this in the definition. If it continues after his physical death, in some way as yet unknown to us, include it. A person's mind is then the entire series of all his states of consciousness. Is this not a simple and sensible way to view the matter?

2. By a person's mind we may also mean whatever it is which makes it immediately possible for him to *have* any states of consciousness or any experiences whatever. It conditions and *stands in back* of his consciousness, so to speak. Certainly he seems to need his body for this purpose; and we shall say more about this in discussing mechanisms.

Now at last we reach our second major question on the conscious mind; as to what its *contents* are. Here psychologists are not in agreement: they simply do not concur as to the various *types* of entities which we find when we "introspect" or examine our own "stream of consciousness" to see what is going on.

Edward B. Titchener (1867-1927) following the lead of the great German "structural" psychologist Wilhelm Wundt (1832-1920), maintained that all our thought-products are various combinations of three basic building-blocks — sensations, images and feelings.

Other schools have denied that this "elementism" or

"content psychology" makes any sense. The behaviorists, for example, say the idea of consciousness itself is meaningless. It gives us, they point out, no help in animal psychology, and in the most of child and abnormal psychology, because reports from the "consciousnesses" of these subjects, via language, is not forthcoming. It is as if they *had* no consciousness, only their actions to speak for them. So why not go along on that basis with everybody, say the behaviorists.

"Act" psychologists such as Brentano, Stumpf, Kulpe and others have also denied that mind can be understood in terms of certain basic elements which it combines and recombines. Their school has developed into the belief in "imageless thought." There are thoughts and acts, they feel, which cannot be resolved into simple components such as sensations, images and feelings.

Another school, that of the "Gestalt" psychologists, goes still further and holds that every mental event and act causes, through creative synthesis, a *new* and *unique quality* to emerge. They feel that to try to analyze mind into any simple elements destroys its very character.

Thus we see that the conscious mind takes a great deal of understanding! It is tempting to dwell longer upon this matter of the actual contents of mind. But we must go on to our last topic in this chapter, one closer to our interests, namely the mechanisms which make consciousness possible.

Here we must note at first a tremendously complicated problem — the true relation between the "mind" and the "body." These seem separate, and, the brain being part of the body, it seems as though therefore a person's *mind* and his *brain* are two distinct entities. We can say, for example, with truth that the two hemispheres of a man's *brain* weigh 1200 grams. Would we be willing to say *his mind* weighs 1200 grams?

Probably not. "Mind" and "brain" each stand for distinct groups of observations. But "there are discoverable regularities, or laws, within each group. There are laws of association, of memory; and there is the structure of the *mind* as revealed by factorial studies. There are, in the other field, laws of neurophysiology, and the regular anatomical structure of the *brain* repeated in each member of a species.

"It is with recent endeavors to unite the two disciplines of psychology and neurology that this book is chiefly concerned." ("The Science Of Mind And Brain," p. 9, by J. S. Wilkie, pub. by Hutchinson's University Library, London, 1953). The above quotation was given to indicate that this "mind vs. brain" problem is widely recognized.

But the moment we conclude that a man's mind and his brain are two different things, we are plagued with the question as to what the relationship is between them — and between a mind and its entire body.

There are five main views: 1. that only the body is of basic reality, the mind being a kind of shadow, offshoot or by-product of the body (materialism) ; 2. that, contrariwise, only mental things are real, and that physical things such as bodies are themselves but *appearances to minds* (idealisms, such as Christian Science) ; 3. that both mind and body are equally real, but that mental events and bodily events run along on parallel lines, like two train-tracks that never meet nor influence one another in the slightest (parallelism) ; 4. that both mind and body are equally real, but that they interact, sometimes the mind causing its body to act, and sometimes the body causing a mental event in the mind connected with it (interactionism, the view of "common sense") ; 5. that mind and body are themselves each merely aspects of a third and underlying reality (neutral monism).

The reader will find it reasonable to suppose that, if only we could discover the true relation between a person's mind and his body (including his brain), we could better appreciate what the conscious mind is. But the "mind-body problem" has never been solved, although most writers on psychiatry, psychology, etc., take sides in the matter.

There are several ways of trying to get further into the problem of consciousness.

The "central theory," e.g., holds that thinking does go on in a real entity called the mind. A stimulus (e.g., a sound wave) arouses in a receptor (e.g., an ear) a nervous impulse which is transmitted to the cerebral cortex (outer covering or "gray matter" of the brain). Here the stimulus is transformed somehow into a thought, or bit of consciousness. We really do have a "mind," in other words, and the brain is its proper organ.

The "central-peripheral" or "motor theory," on the other hand, claims there is no such thing as a separate entity called the mind. This, a mind, is only a *body in action*. What we call "thinking," some say, is only "sub-vocal speech." Thinking is merely "talking to oneself."

Which view is right; and how much of the mind *is* simply the body in action?

If there were a clear-cut, symmetrical, point-for-point relationship between a person's *mental events* and his *bodily events,* knowledge of the conscious mind could be forthcoming. But the complications are staggering.

For example, *some* areas of the body are so equipped that they can carry various sensory messages (of pain, pressure, cold, etc.) to the brain; other areas are not.

Nerves from *some* parts of the body switch over from one side to the other (left to right, or right to left) when ascending from the body-part to the brain, and when descending from the brain to the body-part; other nerves do not switch over. The first kind are called contralateral, the second ipsilateral. Thus (to illustrate one contralateral case) if I get a *sensation* from my right hand, *or* if I decide to *move* my right hand, it is the *left* side of my brain that, as the case may be, either *receives* the sensation from the right hand, or *gives* the order for the right hand to move.

So-called "midline" activities, such as talking, have still a third arrangement. "The vocal cords, the tongue and the lips are bilateral (midline) organs, which are not used in halves but rather all at once. Both sides of them work at once. Also in listening to sounds or in looking at objects we use both ears or both eyes as the case may be. Here the 'cross-over' rule will not work. In all these cases the interesting question is whether we use both sides of our brain or only one." (Physiological Psychology," by Morgan & Stellar, p. 505, Mc Graw-Hill pub., 1950).

We have been talking about the usual situation with animals (including the human), wherein sensations go *to* the brain (usually the cortex) where they somehow get "into" the mind and are interpreted; and wherein orders or willed actions go *from* this same cortex (though from other areas of it) down to the muscles, organs, etc. of the body, where these orders are transformed into motor activities.

There is a further complication here, however, in that this entire situation tends to be represented *upside down*. E.g., the brain area from which an order must go to move, say, the right foot, is at the *very top* of the motor section of the (left hemisphere of the) cerebrum, instead of at its lower end, as we would expect.

How the brain works has been the lifelong study of many great scientists; yet very much more remains to be discovered than ever has been. The specific work of *some* of the parts of the brain (localized functions) is known; of others, unknown. *Some* parts of the brain can *take over* (in time of accident, e.g.) the work of other parts; but the other parts can do only their own type of work.

The *association areas* of the brain are tremendously complex and but slightly understood. Consider, e.g., what occurs in your brain when someone says to you, "Write this address down."

Your auditory mechanism must receive and change those sound waves into nervous impulses and transmit them to a special part of the temporal lobe of your brain, which somehow translates the impulses into the ideas they *mean.* Thus there must be nerve connections between this auditory terminal in your brain and your *word-association* area.

Then the correct nerve-fibres in your brain must be activated between *this* area and the *motor* area which sends orders down into your arm so it can write.

And there must be the correct associations between this motor area and *another* association area which will make sure that your arm muscles write the correct words and no others.

Then your eyes must be able to make another part of your brain (visual association area — Brodmann's "area 18") check what you are writing, so that another part can, if necessary, correct mistakes.

And finally, if you say "Thanks" for that address,

you must issue certain orders to your voice-box muscles — the results of which will, again, be conveyed to your ears and heard by that special part of the temporal lobe of your brain.

This ability to bind together various sensations, acts and ideas into meaningful wholes is called *eugnosia*, and "appears to be a function of association-cortex. Those parts of the cortex adjacent to the primary receptive areas receive fibres from these areas and in turn are connected with each other and with the rest of the cerebral cortex." ("Fundamentals Of Neurology," p. 313, by Dr. Ernest Gardner, pub. by W. B. Saunders Co., 1952).

When things go wrong with these eugnotic functions (that we all take for granted) we have such disorders as "alexia" (inability to *understand* printed language — though the eye still *sees* as well as ever; "astereognosis" (inability to *recognize* objects by touch), etc., etc. An excellent book covering this subject is "Aphasia Therapeutics" by Longerich and Bordeaux published by The Macmillan Co. 1954.

We have gone a little into the complexities of "the conscious mind" because there is a moral to it. We see that mental life is a multi-dimensional manifold of great intricacy, about which, relatively speaking, very little is known.

Yet the mind, and the brain which seems to underlie it, are fascinating awe-inspiring *actualities*. And we *are only on the threshold* of what they *can do* for us. That is the moral of this chapter. *We have only just begun* to think, and to use our mental powers. Let us then keep these wondrous minds of ours open, as we delve further into the subject's mysteries. The author, through the patient years of studying hypnosis and self-hypnosis, has translated some of these *potentialities* into *actualities;* and wants the reader to know what he has discovered.

In developing our next topic, we shall begin to realize the riches that lie in this vast sub-continent, "the subconscious." Our task is to mine these riches, bring them to the surface, and use them for fuller living.

CHAPTER III

The Subconscious Mind

The "subconscious mind" is regarded by some persons as a fanciful entity dreamed up by over-imaginative psychologists, and incapable of "common sense" verification. Consequently it shall be our aim, first, to show that there is a *place* for the subconscious in any reasonable view of human experience. (We mean "place" in a metaphorical sense, of course: perhaps "room" would be a better word.)

Indeed, there are several places. This is the first point we may agree on. After that, there is considerable leeway as to just which and how many of these places, areas or parts of experience constitute the subconscious. But the function itself must certainly be included in any comprehensive view of human nature.

There are five basic reasons for believing in the existence of the subconscious mind — and for being sure each of us has one. These reasons, in our own terminology, and drawn together by our own considerations of the subject, will be referred to as the *a priori*, the *neurological*, the *recording* (or argument from memories), the argument from *unusual states*, and, finally, *unconscious motivation*.

1. The *a priori* argument. "A priori" is Latin for "in

advance of," and refers to the fact that sometimes one can know certain truths in advance of actual happenings. E.g., "you can't make an omelet without breaking eggs." The egg-breaking would be an a priori truth as regards omelet-making.

Now consciousness in itself is a process that is the result of other processes. Anything that passes the *threshold* into consciousness must belong, by definition, to this result. But the result will have to have a cause (*all* results must have causes) which, like itself, may be very complicated, but which, *unlike* itself (by definition) will *not* be conscious. This *necessary* cause of a conscious result is simply what we mean by the subconscious. It *has* to exist, as one can see by analyzing the situation.

When we learn that great psychologists like Wilhelm Wundt have described in careful and convincing detail how a "psychical compound" passes the psychological threshold and goes on into the "field of consciousness" to whatever position of clarity it is destined to occupy momentarily in our conscious life, then moves to the fringe of consciousness, and drops out, as it were, into the limbo of possible memory, we find it easier to envisage the role of the subconscious.

When we read that Paul Schilder, mentioned earlier, reminds us in his book that all recalled *mental objects*, e.g., the remembered sight of a distant house, or a musical theme, must have preparatory work done on them by our physiological and hidden mental processes— which he lumps together and calls the "object function"

— we realize that this work must be "an entirely extra-conscious mechanism."

But last, even *in* our field of consciousness at any one time, we apply the well-known psychological activity called *attention*. This, as we all know, is like nothing so much as a searchlight or spotlight, *around the fringe of which* all the *other* parts of our field of consciousness tend to fade off into the unattended-to. So here, in our first argument, is a *second* legitimate meaning for our concept, "the subconscious mind."

2. The *neurological* argument rests upon the fact, widely known for more than a hundred years by physiologists, neurologists, that the typical nervous action has *three parts* to it, being called the "receptor-connector-effector process." This threefold process known as "the nervous system," is itself within a *wider* threefold process; namely, 1. our entire sensory apparatus (including eyes, ears, taste buds, etc.), 2. the nervous system just mentioned, and 3. our entire effector apparatus (muscles, glands).

The nervous system is always "in the middle" between our sensations and our actions. It too, as stated above, consists naturally of three parts. The first of these, 1. *receives* messages from all the sense organs (hence "receptor"). E.g., the inside wall of the *retina* is part of the receptor organ for vision, and is continuous with the *optic nerve*. The retina is part of our sense apparatus.

The optic nerve, *receiving* the retina's messages, belongs therefore to this first part of our nervous system.

Part 2. of our nervous system is the connector part, which has the job of deciding *how to handle* all the messages given by the sense organs to part 1. E.g., after our brain, correctly interpreting a certain visual percept, enables us to see an oncoming baseball, we might *decide* to duck.

Part 3. of our nervous system would *transmit this message to* the actual effector muscles used to duck with — and would thus join on to them.

How all these junctions are effected is a part of the study of physiological psychology. But enough has been said, we hope, to show that the nervous system has three parts and is itself the middle of three larger parts, since it connects up our senses with our muscles.

We come now to the fascinating point of all this. The connector or middle part of the nervous system, we said, *always has to decide what to do* with its sensory messages, and how, if at all, it will make us act upon them. But, besides the spinal cord, (though it too belongs to the central nervous system), there are no less than *five main middle parts* of the nervous system, *only part of one of which* is regarded as the seat of consciousness! We now begin to see, again, why there is "plenty of room" to believe in the subconscious. For these four and a half, say, out of five middle parts of the nervous system, *though not conscious, are all directing traffic!* It seems to us that anyone who says "the subconscious" is an imaginary idea has a lot of tall explaining to do!

The five main middle parts just referred to are "the five main divisions of the brain ... These five divisions have been selected by neuro-anatomists because they can trace these divisions through the embryological development of the brain." ("Physiological Psychology," p. 38-39.). This indicates to modern biologists that one brain has been *added on* to an earlier one, over the millions of years of evolutionary life. Thus there is present in man a *most rudimentary* brain-part, the first; and a *most highly evolved part,* the last one evolved in time, (only *part* of which, the cerebrum, is the actual "seat of consciousness.")

This cerebrum, or "roof-brain," as the greatest of all neuro-physiologists, Sir Charles Sherrington, calls it, *leaves to the other, lower brain centers the automatic and semi-automatic duties of life.* They are therefore *centers* of these various activities.

The earliest of the five brains, the hindbrain, divides into two parts, the *myelencephalon* (or medulla, which is the center for breathing, heart action, etc.); and the *metencephalon* (containing the cerebellum, center for motor coordinations; and the *pons* or bridge, leading upward to the midbrain.)

The midbrain, called the *mesencephalon,* contains the "colliculi." These nodules are the *primitive* visual and auditory centers for directing, without our attention, our many automatic and subconscious seeing and hearing activities.

The forebrain, in man, divides up into the *diencephalon* (containing, e.g., the thalamus, the great automatic relay station of the brain; and, under it, the hypothalamus, the main center for the entire autonomic — sympathetic and parasympathetic, i.e. — nervous system; and the *telencephalon*) *part* of which consists of the "roof-brain" — cerebral hemispheres — aforementioned.

I think the reader can appreciate the force of the neurological argument for the existence of the subconscious. In lower forms of animals, these, to us, lower brain-forms are, for them, their highest, and would consequently be *their* seats of consciousness. In us, whose roof-brains give us our consciousness proper, the lower brain-units, though active, do not enter consciousness at all, *except* perhaps at unusual times. At any rate, they can be said, taken together, to help form our subconscious mind. There is, again, certainly a *place* for such a mind. Indeed, it is an unavoidable concept.

One last point. If the reader will refer back to our receptor-connector-effector remarks, he can now see that *each* of these *four* lower brain-units is also "in the middle" in the same way as the roof-brain is. For each has to receive sense-messages from *its* receptor mechanisms, "decide" how to handle them, and then issue the appropriate orders to the effector muscles and glands with which *it* normally communicates.

A great deal is known by neurologists about these various nervous pathways. E.g., sensory messages (not usually received into our actual consciousness) from our expanding lungs travel regularly to the medulla where, unbeknown to us, and at a certain point in our inspirational (breathing-in) process, *contrary* orders are issued for us to start breathing-out. When anything goes wrong with this lifelong subconscious stream of messages to the medulla, "the inspiratory centers discharge continuously and the animal dies in a state of prolonged inspiration. Normal respiration is reflexly controlled by modifying the intrinsic activity of these centers." ("Fundamentals Of Neurology," p. 256).

Considering all the automatic activities of our bodies, e.g., digestion and other metabolism, breathing, circulation of blood, winking, regulation of body temperature, etc., it is easy to surmise that, as is thought, our subconscious minds are somehow wider and deeper in extent than are our strictly conscious minds.

3. The *recording* argument for the existence of the subconscious simply refers to the fact that we have *some kind of storehouse* for our host of memories. We *re*-collect a fact by calling it back from this storehouse of memory. Whoever objects to thinking of this vast mysterious warehouse as part of the "subconscious," should tell us what other name he prefers to use for it, and we'll accommodate him. But we certainly need a name for it. The Greeks had one. In their beautiful mythology Mnemos-

yne was the goddess of Memory, mother of the Muses. Our English word comes from the Latin *memoria*.

The term "engram" has been in dictionaries for many years, ever since R. Semon used it to mean a permanently altered state of living tissue — the *physiological* aspect of a "memory." If we do not have actual memories of everything that ever happened to us, we may at least have engrams or physiological traces of them.

But, "Where or how does the brain store its memories?" That is the great mystery. How can learning persist unreproduced,* being affected by other learning while it waits? On the proper occasion what was learned reappears somewhat modified. Where was it in the meantime? The Gestalt psychologists speak of traces which may be altered before they are reproduced. The psychoanalysts speak of the unconscious or the foreconscious where the ideas await call in what Herbart described as a 'state of tendency.'" ("History Of Experimental Psychology," p. 670 by Edwin G. Boring, pub. by Appleton-Century-Crafts, Inc., 1950.)

Now when we remind ourselves that the hypnotist can "regress" his hypnotized subject to go back in time and recall events never consciously remembered before—the truth of which will be proven subsequently herein—we see that there *is* somewhere within us a subconscious area of memories.

4. The argument from *unusual states*, alone, could make two large books. For it refers to the two strange

*i.e., unremembered; sometimes for years.

variants of consciousness called dreams and hypnotic trance. Inasmuch as the latter will be discussed in the chapter "What Is Hypnosis?", we shall consider here only dreams.

To begin with, we have *facts* to *explain*. Dreaming is a worldwide phenomenon, characteristic of the human mind, as we know from historical comments down through antiquity . . . when the dream analyst was usually a person of much prestige and power. Dreams: — what is the explanation of these hallucinations; absurd, fanciful, usually filled with strange visual imagery and erratic actions, often as vivid, real and compelling as our waking moments; often, too, weird, witty, astonishing, fantastically beautiful?

"For those who are awake," said Heraclitus in the 6th century B.C., "only one world exists. During sleep, everyone returns to his own." And in our day Freud defined the dream simply as "the life of the mind during sleep." We read that Freud's "ideas spread until they pervaded all thinking about human motivation both among the psychologists and among the lay public . . . He gave the concept of the unconscious mind to common sense." And which of his many books is "considered to be his greatest work."? The one called "Die Traumdeutung," or "The Interpretation Of Dreams," which he showed to be "the partially concealed expression of repressed wishes." ("A History Of Experimental Psychology," pps. 707 and 710).

Moderns do not believe that dreams represent the activities of evil powers. Nor, when studied, do dreams seem to be a mere senseless play of uncoordinated mental elements, meaningless sequences of images. The leading view against the Freudian theory is the *physiological* view, that dreams are *misinterpretations* of sensory impressions (Lydiard H. W. Horton), as when a student with an earache dreams of thunderstorms; or are *elaborations* of such stimuli, by free association of ideas (Harry L. Hollingworth). The latter experimented with sleeping student-subjects: — when made to breathe perfume, one began dreaming of entering a perfumer's shop in Cairo, etc. A. Maury, because a bed-board hit the back of his neck, dreamed in full circumstance about being guillotined in the French Revolution.

Freud himself discussed this physiological theory of dreams, analyzed it carefully and concluded that "sensory stimuli may be starting-points for dream material, but they are not the motives; the latter are to be found in the personality of the dreamer." ("Abnormal Psychology," by Raleigh M. Drake, David McKay Co., pub., 1936). The energy for dreams is supplied by "a great many deeply repressed childhood wishes — waiting for an occasion to penetrate" to consciousness. ("Medical Psychology," p. 218).

Our logical position is, then, that if the unusual mental state called dreaming is to be seen as an argument for the existence of the subconscious mind, it must *lead back to* and uncover that mind — show us that such a mind exists, and show us *what it is doing.*

Though it is notoriously difficult to analyze dreams, still, (as Freud observed), if a child keeps his fist so tightly clenched that it can scarcely be opened, we do not take this to mean "there's nothing in it." And so with dreams. There is a dream-technique, not that of the cheap "dream-books," the old-fashioned superstitious oneirology which regarded a dream as a *portent* or prophecy (of the future). The correct analysis goes *backward* in time; the dream means something in terms of the dreamer's *past*: — an entirely different, modern approach.

Here is the gist of what we need for grasping it. Most psychiatrists use dream-analysis as an *aid* in understanding patients. These experts look first for the "primary effect" of a dream . . . the dominant emotion in it, e.g., terror, anger, horror, sex excitement. They then study the "symbolism" of the dream. Here we find an interesting situation. If the dream expresses the subconscious, as we believe, it will be revealing an *earlier part of the mind* which will have *its own kind of language*. Dreams are an *utterance* of the subconscious which represents, in human history, a time long prior to the use of *modern* language.

To see that this makes sense, let us reflect that most of our *abstract* words in use today were originally *concrete*, this early significance having faded. Thus "tumult" comes from the (Latin) word meaning a "swelling,"; and so, etymologically, for thousands of examples, regardless of the original languages borrowed from. E.g., to dissipate meant to throw; humble meant on low ground;

luminary meant an actual shining light; queer meant oblique or slanting; barbarous meant not Greek. Some words retain *both* their earlier concrete (referring to the physical fact itself) and their later abstract (referring to qualities or properties only) meanings. E.g., "crooked" still means *both* not straight (concrete meaning) and dishonest (abstract meaning).

We repeat, dreams come from a prehistoric level of the mind and will *naturally* be expressed in their own, strangely concrete, "primordial language," which will not be our language of today. *Therefore* we must interpret dream-language into today's language, so we can understand it. With practice, facility is gained, and the whole thing begins to make sense.

For example, if you *pick something up* in a dream, this might mean you are *choosing* it. In other words, you can't *dream* choosing, you somehow have to act it out. This all-important symbolism in dreams usually comes in the form of visual imagery. Freud thought this set of symbols was the same for everyone:* but many analysts, starting with Freud's disciple, the brilliant Wilhelm Stekel, believe that every dreamer has to some extent his own symbols.

At any rate, *several* dreams from an individual, especially instances of a *recurring* dream, can guide experts with astonishing frequency to what is called "the life conflict."

---

*Other analysts agree. E.g., "the universality of dream symbols is . . . uncontestable; we have reason to assume that it is only one of the broad layers of psychological life common to all people. Just as body-structures and body-functions are universal, so too are certain psychological functions." ("Medical Psychology," p. 223).

Much of the symbolism of dreams appears, even to an intelligent amateur, to make good sense. He is prepared to believe that falling into an abyss, in a dream, may mean lack of self-confidence; that a closed door indicates frustration, or a secret; a convent, fear of love or sex; a net, a dilemma; a museum, the mind; etc.

In dreaming, the intellect shows both surprising power, and considerable limitation. E.g., as to the former, we must admit wonderingly that the mind *creates all of the characters* in the dream, and all of the events, however bizarre both may be. You unconsciously construct dreams "wholly out of material from within yourself. You figure in them either as an apparent spectator or as an actual participant — and in psychological reality you are both, even though one or more of the characters wear masks of other identities. When a character in your dreams appears as mother, father, sister, brother, friend or enemy, it is you portraying the role with the naturalness of an accomplished actor. You even convince yourself that the protagonist with whom you are matching wits is authentic. A Barrymore could not do more!" ("How To Understand Your Dreams," by Wilhelm Stekel, pub. by Eton Books, Inc., 1951).

The subconscious mind is here an amazing dramatist. Mark Twain called it "the dream-artist who resides in us," and "the mysterious mental magician." He thought dreams actually had a higher reality than our waking moments. "Everything in a dream is more deep and strong and sharp than is ever its pale imitation in the unreal life which is ours when we go about awake and clothed with our artificial selves." (from "My Platonic Sweetheart," Readers Digest, Nov. 1953).

As for limitations, one is that the dream-mind does not possess connective words like "but," "therefore," "and," "because," etc. It can't *dream* them. They therefore must be supplied, if at all, by the waking mind when interpreting the dream. Their lack, in our dreams, helps to explain why the latter seem so chopped up, with such abrupt changes and unrelated episodes.

Very well, assume that an expert correctly interprets a dream (translates the "manifest content" into the "latent content") : — *what does it show* the subconscious mind doing? Answer: — the dream is the art product, so to speak, of the subconscious mind, and shows it *providing a temporary solution to a problem or wish.* Any civilized being is, in part, uncivilized. Granted? This latter part, the *id* (Freud) has antisocial desires (e.g., for sexual promiscuity, violent revenge upon persons who are partly, at least, hated; etc.). All such desires are successfully repressed during waking hours by the thoughtful, civilized part of our natures (ego) ; but they press for some kind of expression or utterance when we are relaxed, during sleep (one-third of our lives). Even then, however, the *ego* part of us is like a censor half awake, and succeeds in getting our "naked" desires clothed in the symbolism of the dream.

Freud said an unfulfilled wish is like a ghost that continues to walk until redeemed. Our dreams, whether understood by us or not, express those wishes which are destined, for most of us, to remain otherwise unexpressed.

But here comes an objection to the theory. Many dreams are *unpleasant*. How then can they represent an *expression* of our wishes? Do we *want* to hurt ourselves deliberately by constantly manufacturing p a i n f u l dreams? No: the answer to this riddle is as follows: the repressed wish is so strong that it would awaken the relaxed, "off guard" sleeper unless he got a *substitute satisfaction* in the dream — which therefore protects him from awakening! It keeps him asleep. And so we arrive at Freud's theory that all dreams are wish-fulfilments. (They are flagrantly self-serving. "The good," said Plato, "are those who content themselves with dreaming of what the wicked actually do.")

Many seeming exceptions to this theory prove, upon adequate analysis, to fall into line. Thus one lady told Freud about a dream in which she wished to give a dinner, but was prevented in several ways. "How was *that* wish-fulfilment?" she asked. Freud elicited the further facts that the dreamer's husband was very fond of a certain woman — who was, however, too thin for his fancy. *Her* favorite dish was smoked salmon — which was exactly what the lady, in her dream, could not procure for dinner! The dreamer had made a dream in which her desire that her potential rival not become any *more* desirable was fulfilled.

Space lacks to discuss other main mechanisms of dreams, such as condensation, dramatization, displacement, secondary elaboration, projection, identification. To see how dreams are analyzed, one may read a book like Stekel's "How To Understand Your Dreams," filled with hundreds of examples.

The present writer has collected and catalogued many dreams, and wishes there were space to do more than mention a few. There are many examples of the sex type of dream, with its obvious symbolism.

There is the "death wish" dream, vehemently denied by the dreamer, when told that at least a part of him wants or once wanted someone, usually a relative, dead or removed. When we realize that we are usually *ambivalent* toward those close to us, both hating them (for reasons we don't acknowledge) and loving them, the "death wish" dream seems not ridiculous — for we have repressed this hate-aspect, and it can come out only in the dream. Thus with "unconscious hypocrisy" the dreamer deplores the death of the loved (and hated) one, trying usually *unsuccessfully* to save him.

The opposite wish too can be dreamed. "When a man has lost someone dear to him," says Freud, "for a considerable period afterwards he produces a special type of dream, in which the most remarkable compromises are effected between his knowledge that that person is dead, and his desire to call him back to life." (General Introduction To Psychoanalysis," p. 196).

Here follows a verbatim report of such a dream, from a student of mine. "I eloped twenty years ago and my husband was killed the next day in a car accident. I was injured and was unable to go to the funeral. For the next fifteen years I would dream of him coming to me and telling me he wasn't killed, and he'd go into detail about the funeral, in which he very cleverly sneaked out of the casket. I wanted very much to go back with him, but he would tell me that I didn't love him as I had married another, and would walk away. Then I would wake up crying. After fifteen years of practically the same dream on the average of once every two months, he finally told me in the last dream that he was really dead and wanted me to be happy."

We said dreams are to be understood as wishes of the subconscious layers of our personalities, rather than as prophecies. One important type of dream is, however, both — namely, those warning of impending mental illness. Such coming maladies are often foreshadowed by typical, representative dreams.

A person inclined towards obsessional delusions (fixed ideas) may dream of something happening over and over, e.g., a fish swimming around in a glass bowl. A threatening confusion of thoughts ("flight of ideas") may be dreamed recurrently as some confusion of insects or other things. A person threatened with schizophrenia — which, if contracted, will make it difficult to stay in touch with the real world and play his part in it — may dream of being wheeled around in a perambulator.

Dreams "are invariably useful for demonstrating hidden negative attitudes toward psychotherapy." E.g., "Dreams of self-destruction are frequently reported" by a certain type of patient and, "if discussed from the self-punishment aspect, dangerous acting-out may be prevented." (Specialized Techniques In Psychotherapy," ed. by Bychowski and Despert, p. 311, pub. by Basic Books, Inc. 1952).

Dreams may "play a very useful role in emergency psychotherapy. If they occur regularly enough they are the best guide to the current unconscious problems of the patient." (ibid., p. 329).

We said there were five strong reasons for believing in the existence of the subconscious mind; and have discussed four of them. The first three belong together, referring especially to the unvarying, general *structure* and *functioning* of the mind. The *a priori* argument pointed out that the subconscious represents certain necessary *preconditions* of consciousness. The *neurological* argument is based upon the organization of the nervous system, with its five brain divisions. The *recording* argument, referring to memory, is again based on facts universally known and admitted. These three arguments refer to *usual* situations.

The fourth argument, from analysis of the *unusual states* of dreams and hypnotism, has been divided into the treatment just completed on dreams, and into a later chapter on hypnosis.

The fifth argument is on *unconscious motivation*, which not only falls between usual and unusual mental events — being sometimes one and sometimes the other — but is of special importance to the reader. To it, therefore, we now turn.

CHAPTER IV
Subconscious Motivation

The best way to appreciate, logically, the role of subconscious motivation is to remember that a motive is a type of *cause*, the action that results therefrom being the *effect* of the cause. In the type we are considering there is a difference of both *time* and *place* between the cause and its result: of time, because a cause must always occur before its result; of place, because the motive is in the subconscious part of the mind — hence the chapter title — whereas the result is in consciousness.

That a person often does not — because he cannot inspect his subconscious — know the true cause of his action or belief, can be a big problem. But he does know the result; and he likes to *think* he knows the cause. Often he assigns a noble or praiseworthy cause or reason for some action of his. This is called *rationalization*, a process which to some extent we all indulge in.

Too often, the real, subconscious reason for an act was ignoble rather than noble. An outside observer can frequently spot the true, ignoble reason for the act, whereas the person himself can see only his spurious, assumed reason. If we reflect on this situation for a few minutes, we shall realize the force of this fifth argument for the existence of the subconscious mind. At times we can almost *see* it working in others, who are themselves unaware of it.

Let us give a few examples, so we can appreciate the many ways in which subconscious motives "get into the act."

Case 1. A poor boy, brought up "on the wrong side of the tracks," managed to get through college by living with an indigent aunt and working long hours at night in a factory, under a gruff and cruel boss. The girl he met at college and fell in love with was very popular, but she returned his love, believed in him, and after graduation they married.

In a couple of years, though she was extremely unselfish, and a devoted wife and mother, he began to ignore her pointedly in public, and then to treat her insultingly in front of others. Their mutual friends, embarrassed, stopped associating with them. She was bewildered and hurt, and felt their marriage would end in divorce. What was wrong here?

Ans. Any explanation the husband could have given for his treatment of her — that she was "dumb," or whatever — would have been rationalization. His real motive was subconscious. If his subconscious mind could have delivered a speech, it would have gone like this: "All my life I've been a nobody. I've had to keep regarding myself as *inferior* in background, social class, opportunity, income, etc. *Now* I'm going to experience the relief and luxury of·seeing myself as *superior*. I can do this most easily by degrading my wife; she's the only one around that will 'take it.' My superiority is easily achieved, being a relative matter, caused by making *her* look *inferior*. Naturally I'm not going to admit this to myself consciously. I'll just enjoy the situation to the fullest, without understanding it."

Thus, we see, the subconscious *has effects, unsuspected,* on the conscious mind.

Case 2. The youngest of five brothers, teased and tormented by them, was brought up with special attention and devotion by his understanding mother. She conquered his shyness with girls, taught him to dance, etc. He called her his best girl. When a young man, he went with a girl five years older than he was, who resembled his plain mother; and with a pretty girl three years younger, who thrilled him very much physically. For some reason unknown to him, he married the older girl. A year later, meeting the younger one, he brought her home to dinner. As the weeks passed, he tried to have her around all the time, and, when his wife resented it, flew into a rage, calling her unreasonable, jealous of all his friends, etc. What is the situation here?

Ans. Unconscious motivation again. He was *always* more attracted to the younger woman, but married the older one because she was a mother substitute who made him feel secure. Then later, subconsciously, he was trying to get for himself *both* maternal security and amatory satisfaction. His conscious, made-up motive toward the younger woman was innocent friendship. His wife sensed his real motive and, legitimately, was troubled and indignant. Such a marriage could go on the rocks because of this one hidden motive.

Case 3. As a child, Mary always felt unwanted, unloved, neglected. Growing up, she vowed that no child of hers would be so lonely and unhappy. She married and had a son, whose schedule of activities and discipline she thought out and applied with great thoroughness. She prided herself on being loving and devoted, "a perfect mother." But to her astonishment she found that the rigid routine she set for the boy aroused his increasing resistance. He wanted to play in his own way; and was, daily, harder and harder to control. As he grew up, he showed increasing defiance, then even hatred of her — and usually before guests. Of course she was crushed by the boy's "ingratitude." What was the situation here?

Ans. As the boy grew up, she was using him to enjoy a subconscious revenge upon her mother. This case is a little harder to see, as it involves our realizing the recurrent phantasy-life in which Mary, in effect, kept imagining she was telling *her* mother, "I'll show *you* how a child should be raised. The way I'm raising my boy is the way *you* should have raised *me;*" etc. This bitterness came out in harshness and arbitrariness of control over the boy, whose normally developing self-expression was hampered, and who grew to detest the cause of it — his mother. Actually, her control was motivated by hatred rather than by love. That she was the perfect, devoted mother was a rationalization of an unworthy, subconscious motive. This, again, could ruin a life or lives. Louis Bromfield's novel, "A Good Woman," shows how much harm such concealed motivation can do, and how hard it is to discover.

Case 4. A girl, the youngest of six children, is always pushed into the background. Also, she grows up wearing the hand-me-down or cast-off clothing of the others, never having anything that's really her own. Striving subconsciously for the status and social recognition which all personalities young and old, require for happiness, she finds she can attract attention by being a "tomboy." But as she grows older she realizes the attention she thereby achieves is not the kind she wants. For a tomboy as such is a kind of freak, *not* respected for her femininity, and *as a woman*. But recognition of any kind has never come to her unbidden; she has secured all of it she ever had by *over-acting*. So, to attract attention as a woman, she becomes "daring," even promiscuous. Ultimately she falls deeply in love with a certain man — who, when he learns of her reputation, begins to treat her accordingly. She repulses him, for she craves his genuine respect. This he cannot feel for her: and he goes out of her life for good. All love and faith die in her, and she becomes wilder, lonelier than ever.

Here we already have the analysis; we see, again, that a subconscious motivation, perhaps forever unsuspected, can ruin a life. The subconscious cause has destructive conscious effects.

Case 5. Our last case illustrates the type of situation in which analysts have to "go deeper" to find the solution. A girl is brought up by a maiden aunt who must go to work daily. The girl thus comes home from school to a dark empty house, to which she lets herself in by a key worn on a string around her neck. She envies her girl friends who come home to waiting mothers. But she is known for being always pleasant and composed; and for being very generous — though *she* will never accept gifts from *others*. She meets a young man who falls in love with her, though her strange self-sufficiency puzzles him. He gives her an expensive necklace, which she seems to appreciate. Then he learns to his horror that she has given it away to a poor girl of her acquaintance. Her offhand explanation that she had other jewelry and so could spare it, fails to soothe his feelings. He decides sadly that she has no real affection for him; and breaks up with her.

Did she give the necklace away because it reminded her of "the key?"

No: she would have given it away anyway. The answer lies deeper. Not having, in her girlhood, the things that meant security to other girls, she had carefully, though subconsciously, built up a false self-sufficiency over the years, which expressed itself in her *never seeming to need anything*. She "sold" this to herself by giving things to others, but refusing to accept in return. And she masked her hidden loneliness with the pleasant, calm exterior. The trouble went still deeper; for she *generalized* the situation, becoming afraid of all normal social needs. This type of person is apt to pretend great self-sufficiency, maintaining (rationalization again) that close personal ties lead only to painful obligations and inevitable disillusionments. Actually, they shy away from close ties because they just have no experience with and technique for handling them.

This case, like Case 1, is an example of "reaction formation," in which a person reacts by making the pendulum swing too far the other way. Thus, in Case 1, a person who has felt very inferior compensates by acting *too* superior. In Case 5, a person who really craves close ties reacts by cultivating a personality which systematically *rejects* them.

Enough has been said to see how subconscious motives may operate in a person's conscious life: — and we have our fifth reason for believing in a "subconscious." We note that in all of the above cases, a person *wanted* something: in Case 1, it was a feeling of self-respect and worth; in Case 2, a genuine amatory attachment; in Case 3, a kind of vicarious revenge; in Case 4, approval of others; in Case 5, a feeling of security.

Such a person need never *verbalize* his want: he need never say to himself, "What I lack is a feeling of security; and one way or another I'm going to get it." Nevertheless he sets about trying to *satisfy* the want; and *the way he does it*, consciously or subconsciously, is extremely important for his welfare.

The *most striking* method of *implanting* a subconscious motive, though undoubtedly the least frequent, is *post-hypnotic suggestion,* in which, when a person is in a state of hypnosis, it is suggested to him by the hypnotist that the subject do or say or think something specific at a certain time after resuming normal consciousness. It is also suggested that, though he perform the post-hypnotic act, he completely forget it was ever suggested. Instances are legion in which such suggestions are duly carried out, though the reasons for doing them, the motives, are forgotten as ordered. Here we have a perfect case of subconscious suggestion. *These can, therefore, be incorporated into one's life!* But more of this later.

There are *several ways* in which these subconscious motives can be discovered: for example, by "free association," a verbal method perfected by Carl Jung; and through "projective techniques" such as "thematic apperception" and the Rorschach test. As for the latter, Hermann Rorschach, a Swiss psychiatrist (1884–1922), devised ten cards, each containing an elaborate inkblot. Five blots are in color, five in gray and black. Subjects study one blot at a time, and tell the analyst what each blot resembles. The blots are all *deliberately ambiguous,* so that the subject can import his own *meanings* into them as he seeks to explain and describe them. These meanings, in turn, reveal to the analyst *the subconscious ways in which we interpret things,* and the subconscious *motives* so powerful in forming our personalities and moulding our very lives.

Experts can tell a great deal about a person from his Rorschach responses, the main criteria being three: namely, whether the reaction is to the entire blot or to a part; to what extent color, form and movement are seen and imagined; and whether the blots suggest human, animal or inanimate objects.

"Seeing whole figures indicates high intelligence and ability to synthesize. A predominance of forms in motion, especially of human forms, signifies vivid imagination. Great response to color means impulsiveness, if not emotional instability. Seeing mostly animals, and giving unoriginal responses in general, suggest lower intelligence and stereotyped thinking," etc. (Basic Teachings Of The Great Psychologists," by S. Stansfeld Sargent, p. 145, pub. by New Home Library, 1944).

Why do we want to know a person's subconscious motivations? Because such knowledge permits us frequently to analyze them, and so to control and to change them when they are wrong. To remind us as to how they can be wrong, we need only refer back to the five cases. One interesting way to think of wrong or unfortunate subconscious motivations is to see that they limit our free will. Suppose we are motivated, for reasons unknown to us, to act in harmful ways. We would not choose these ways of acting if we understood the situation; therefore our ignorance is limiting our power of choice — our free will. Much of the power of psychotherapy resides in the surprising fact that often, when we see *why* we act as we do, and wish to change our ways, we can.

Neurotic and other poor ways of acting are frequently due to what we might call *logical tragedies*. They are habits which should never have been formed. Such malformation, so to speak, came about in the following way: one event, *A*, was followed by another, *B*, and — regardless of whether *A* actually caused *B* or not, a *habit* was begun in the individual of thinking of, or experiencing *B* whenever *A* occurred thereafter.

For example let us say a five year old child, cutting something with scissors or knife, is startled by a clap of thunder. His hand slips and he cuts himself. There is a great to-do, his finger bleeds, his mother scolds, the entire experience is painful, and the child feels nausea. We tend to forget painful experiences, but our nervous system stores them in the subconscious. Even through the adulthood of this person, whenever he hears thunder, he may experience nausea. He may have forgotten the incident, and will therefore be mystified at the connection, in his "psychology," between thunder and a sick feeling. If he can be made to recall the occasion, the connection (his habit) may be broken. There is no logical tie between many such sequences, which is why it is a tragedy for persons to act, year after year, as though there were.

Some of these habits, therefore, are unfortunate. Now there is no doubt a continual, vitally important series of communications between our conscious and our subconscious minds! When we are *forming* a habit, the direction seems to be from the conscious to the subconscious, for we have to learn the habit by remaining aware of it while we are training our nervous systems. When we are *acting habitually*, however, the direction seems to be the opposite, from the subconscious to the conscious; for to the extent that the habit is really ours, we don't need to keep thinking about it, and can let part of our subconscious take over. When we see a baby learning to walk, we can be sure he is conscious of his lesson. After he has learned, he can walk for miles without thinking of it. So with all habits.

A person's conscious mind is observable — by himself — directly (introspection); and with great clarity, relatively. But his subconscious mind, as we have seen, is not observable directly. Its existence has to be inferred. But this is no reason for us to disbelieve in it. Astronomers tell us that the moon never shows its other side to us, the existence of which we can therefore only infer; but common sense tells us it *must* have another side. This is the way it is too with the subconscious mind. We have seen many reasons to believe in it.

Now in order for us to discover *helpful causal relationships* between the conscious and subconscious minds of each of us, let us briefly examine different methods of psychotherapy. They will give us needed light.

CHAPTER V

Schools of Psychotherapy

"Clinics and consultation-departments will be built, to which analytically oriented physicians will be appointed, so that the men who would otherwise give way to drink, the women who have nearly succumbed under the burden of privations, the children for whom there is no choice but running wild or neurosis, may be made by analysis able to resist and able to do something in the world."

This was Freud's vision, in 1918, of a new social institution, available to all, which saved people whenever possible, *before* they cracked up. How important is it to have such an institution? "About half of the hospital beds in the country are occupied by mental patients, and approximately one out of every twenty persons spends part of his life in a mental institution. This does not mean that mental disorders are more prevalent than physical illnesses, but that mental disease is generally more difficult to cure and therefore requires hospitalization for a longer period of time. Actually, only about one percent of the population is incapacitated on any one day by mental disorders." ("Psychology And Life," p. 198, 4th ed., by Floyd L. Ruch, pub. by Scott, Foresman & Co., 1953, quoting L. Dublin in "Facts Of Life From Birth To Death.")

But to have psychotherapy readily and inexpensively available is still more important than the quotation just above would indicate. This is because every *normal* person can also benefit from psychotherapy, including the reader of this book — who indeed would not be reading it unless he believed this. There are said to be about 500,000 *psychotics* (schizophrenia, manic-depressive and paranoia are the three great functional psychoses) and eight to ten million *neurotics* (obsessions, compulsions, irrational fears, forms of technical hysteria, and "nervous exhaustion" are the main neuroses) in the United States. Yet these total only about six percent of our population. The rest of us, 94 percent, can also be helped.

Nearly everyone will agree that, insofar as they can be meaningfully separated out, mental ills are as serious, and their cure as important, as physical ills. Now the existence of these mental ills is *a matter of degree,* in two very important senses.

First, any such ill can be serious or mild. Thus, though each of the three great functional psychoses mentioned can be so grave as to incapacitate and hospitalize a person, each of them can also exist in a mild form so that a therapist can correctly characterize a person as of "schizoid," "manic" or "paranoid" *type.*

Second, mental illness may be present in *some* degree in every person. It may not be serious, but let no one think he is immune, or free; this is a modern "holier than thou" attitude which we must condemn in the interests of truth.

Let us now take, very briefly, six cases of mental disorder; different types ranging from the very serious to the mild, so that we can appreciate this fact — *the problem of psychotherapy is universal.*

1. A young man's ego-structure is so shattered that he feels his entire personality is not only worthless but a thing to be *avoided at all costs.* How can he do this? By an extreme "withdrawal" called, technically, catatonic schizophrenia. In many such cases contact with this hospital patient cannot be established at all! He may have to be forcibly fed, etc. His arms can be placed in queer, normally uncomfortable positions where they will remain for hours ("waxy" or "lead-pipe flexibility"). He may feel no pain at being pricked with a needle, etc. The chances today are about fifty-fifty that this person can be helped. Skilled psychotherapy can rebuild his ego-structure so he will *want to return* to his self!

2. A young married woman seeks therapy because she has a strange, painful combination of fears (phobias) and compulsions. She has become increasingly afraid to leave her house for any purpose. She is repelled by all shows of affection from her husband. She suffers such mysterious and unrelieved anxiety that she is afraid of going mad. She has recounted her symptoms so often to friends and her husband that she has lost them, and is threatened by him with divorce. Worst of all, she is sure her heart will stop pumping *unless she keeps counting its beats.*

This case, reported at length in "Personality And Psychotherapy," (pps. 16-21, 182-184, etc., by Dollard & Miller, pub. by McGraw-Hill Book Co., Inc., 1950) was effectively unraveled by the psychiatrist on the case. This would have been impossible without eliciting the woman's history. It showed that her sex desires were very strong but had been branded, in her infancy, as disgusting and loathsome by an ignorant mother. This *conflict* between amatory *desire* and *fear* went on entirely in her subconscious: the *results* came out in her strange symptoms. When she kept counting her heartbeats (an operation requiring much attention), it relieved her of much of the anxiety, misery and fear felt by such pronounced neurotics. She kept off of the streets as much as possible because, when she failed to do so, she *tried* — and sometimes succeeded — to get into situations where she would be "taken advantage of" by strange men. (She would ask rides from truck-drivers, etc.) Thus she *could not blame herself* for what happened; something she could not say if she accepted her husband's attentions freely. Her cure lay in her learning how the sex urge-fear linkage was originally formed, and how it explained her hidden conflict. Then she slowly returned to a normal family and social life.

This was a case of serious illness which *fell just short* of need for hospitalization.

3. A certain brilliant man, whose intellect and education are sufficient for him to have debated in New York City with one of the world's leading psychologists,

writes one book after another. But the public never gets a chance to read them, for, unfailingly, as each book is completed, the author finds some reason to become disgusted with the book — which, when he is thoroughly enraged, he hurls savagely into the fire.

This man is wealthy, and does not need revenue from his books. His destruction is "hurting only himself," (which cannot be said of Case 2.). Also, he is in all other respects a normal, charming person. The destructive author has no desire to be analyzed. Either he does not think it necessary ("My next book I *won't* throw into the fire"), or analysis is too painful for him to consider. But can the reader doubt there is something definitely wrong with this man, this brilliantly reasoning irrationalist, which psychotherapy might very well clear up? Meanwhile, society may be losing an invaluable thinker.

4. This case was an only child, male, brought up by a divorced mother. Being of an outwardly gracious but strongly opinionated and domineering type, the mother expressed herself by "topping" whatever the boy did. Not only did "mother know best" but she never allowed the boy to complete anything, coming in at the eleventh hour to put the finishing touch to everything he attempted. Moderns can see how this boy might grow up with the *subconscious feeling* that he could never finish anything — which *generalized* quite naturally to "never be a success." And he wasn't. Having been robbed consistently of little achievemental successes along the way

(these are called "closures"), he had formed a strong habit of *thinking in terms of failure*. "I keep feeling *just as though* I'm under a curse," he would say.

As an adult he took to drinking, not steadily but irregularly; and, when he did, heavily. Under the early-stage exhilaration and general anesthesia of alcohol, his sense of restraint and foredoom-to-failure fell away and he felt "free." He realized that the long-range disadvantages of drinking outweigh its short-range advantages. Then he also began to understand the childhood "smother" pattern of which he was a product. Both realizations took years, but finally he saw his problems. He perceived that he didn't *need* to feel foredoomed to failure; and that for his own good he must switch himself over to feeling predestined to success. But as long as he kept drinking, he was confirming this old escape-pattern.

For a long time, though, he could not stop drinking. When the urge came every few days, it proved too strong to resist. He had some knowledge of psychotherapy and he set to work analyzing the situation. Though only an occasional drinker, he was surprised to discover *how frequent* were the thoughts he had about drinking, the little compulsions to drink which he dismissed because *it wasn't time yet*; (not till the end of the week, etc.). He figured he must be pushing these little compulsions down into his subconscious, and that there they "summated" — added themselves together. When a good time came to drink, they reappeared in full force as *one strong urge,* for which he failed to provide, as an opponent, a superior counter-urge. He figured that the logical way to handle this situation was *not* to try to create one superior counter-urge, but to destroy *each* of the little compulsions as it came up from time to time. *Whenever* one did, therefore, he *immediately* made himself think of all the well-known disutilities of drinking, especially the decrease in physical well-being from the hangover, as this is sensory and easily imagined. Thus there never were a lot of little compulsions stored up in his subconscious so they could pop out as one strong compulsion. When a convenient time came for this man to drink, he now felt, along with a slight immediate urge to do so, a definite sense of nausea. Instead of having *no champion* to fight a *strong* compulsion, he *had* a champion (synthetic, but strong enough) to fight a *weak compulsion.*

This is our first case of a man with quite a serious problem, which he solved by *self-therapy.* He *used* psychology.

5. This type of case is relatively simple, and milder. It's about a man who has a beastly temper, but only on occasion. His wife points out to him that it is only on certain days, when he comes home, that he "makes the family's life miserable." The man is basically good-hearted and kind, as well as thoughtful. So he too begins analyzing, and discovers that, unfailingly, whenever he has "a hard day at the office," — and some of them, in the nature of his work, are very exasperating

— he takes it out on his family. He transfers his frustration and bitterness to them; a phenomenon which we all know, and which is called "displacement." As soon as he realizes this, he forms, slowly and not easily, the habit of treating his family with kindness after his tough days.

6. Our last case is still milder. A woman's friend points out to her that she is *always* late for appointments. The friend has been annoyed by this for a long time, and finally speaks her mind. "Why are you *always* late, year after year, for all dates and appointments?" The woman has to admit this is true; and is mystified. Why *is* she always a little late for everything?

She happens to be going to a psychiatrist on another matter, and asks him about this. He suggests it is her "harmless" way of expressing a subconscious rebellion against authority. "Ridiculous" as this explanation seems at first blush — the history of science is filled with discoveries at first thought ridiculous — the psychiatrist has little difficulty in showing her the hidden causal connection. Her authoritative father had always made her be prompt to the minute — although children need a little time usually to adjust to orders and requests. She had resolved, subconsciously, to assert herself against *all* demands to *appear* someplace and *do* something at *one certain* time. She saw now that it gave her a real "kick" to be a little bit late for everything. She was getting back at her father, but didn't realize it. (Those of us who still say "Ridiculous" to such explanations would probably admit wars as ridiculous too — to say the least. Yet they've been very much matters of fact for thousands of years; and only now do we see some hope of ending them).

These six cases have been presented, we repeat, to make one essential point, that the need for psychotherapy is universal. "Psyche" comes from Greek mythology: she was "a maiden beloved by Cupid; often represented as a young girl with the wings of a butterfly;" being now a "personification of the soul." So it means the soul or mind. "Therapy" comes from the Greek "therapeutes," meaning attendant. Psychotherapy, then, is what ministers to the mind, keeping it healthy or making it so.

How many basic ways are there of ministering to the mind? Each writer seems to have his own classification. But there is no clearcut principle dividing the various schools; for each may show characteristics which distinguish some of the others. Keeping this in mind, let us mention eight schools.

1. *Psychoanalytic*. This stresses the importance of the *early years* in forming personality; and uses the techniques of *dream analysis* and *free association*. The latter refers to letting the patient ramble on and on in his talking, under the sound theory that he cannot honestly refrain from starting to talk about what really bothers him — and thus giving the analyst a key to the patient's troubles.

[74]

This school believes that *transference* results from such interviews. That is, the patient will develop either an affectionate or a hostile attitude toward his analyst, deriving in either case from earlier relations of the patient with one or both of his parents. Such transference of course creates added problems.

The three great figures of this school are Sigmund Freud, Carl G.Jung and Alfred Adler. Freud, the founder, and called — rightly, the author believes — the "Darwin of the mind" — wrote copiously on "depth psychology" from 1880 to 1939. He held that the growing child passes through three main stages (oral, anal, genital), during which different bodily areas and functions are emphasized, causing for him characteristic social problems. If the solutions to these problems are not correctly learned — due usually to parental misguidance — neurotic fixations (lack of normal psychological growth) occur which can cause maladjustments and breakdowns later. Freud also believed there is a stage in most children's lives in which each prefers the opposite-sexed parent to his other parent (Oedipus and Electra "complexes") ; and that failure to develop normally through this stage also causes trouble.

Jung broadened Freud's emphasis on the sex urge (libido) to mean one's general urge to enjoy all pleasures, especially social. To his master Freud's emphasis on the *individual* subconscious mind, Jung added a strong belief in the *racial unconscious,* by which he meant *inherited* dispositions that each person has toward human and subhuman ways of thinking. Jung, still alive at the time of this writing, has developed a *controlled* association technique, now taken over in police "lie detecting." He also thinks a personality is composed of a pattern of opposite qualities, such as thoughts versus feelings, extrovert (outgoing) vs. introvert (indwelling) mental tendencies, etc. A neurotic is a person who has allowed one such tendency to develop out of proportion to the others.

Adler, another of Freud's great pupils, finally rejected his emphasis upon the subconscious, repression, and the overweening force of the sex drive. Instead, Adler was impressed by a person's "will to power" as he grows up, and the "inferiority complex" which results from his failure to achieve power. Adlerian analysts try to discover a person's "style of life" — the ways in which he either tries to secure power and success, pretends he has, or accepts substitutes for them.

A second division that can be made among psychotherapists comprises usually the *non*-psychoanalysts; though not necessarily. This is divided into schools of *directive* and *non-directive* therapy. The former are termed "counselor-centered" because the therapist directs the talking; the latter, "client-centered" because the patient is given little or no direction.

2. *Directive therapy* or counseling is the kind usually given by community agencies, physicians, ministers,

teachers, social workers, lawyers, employment interviewers, friends, etc. In the professional literature it is best represented by the work of Adolph Meyer ("The Common Sense Psychiatry of Dr. Adolf Meyer," Alfred Lief, ed., McGraw-Hill Book Co., Inc., N.Y.1948). Meyer and his followers stress more heavily than do the Freudians the factors of social experience and learning. They stress the patient's entire *present* environment, trying to view him as a whole in terms of what they call "psychobiology." They emphasize *direct instruction* of the patient, and set up manufactured situations for him in which he will have to use certain reconditioning habits valuable in his cure. The results of each interview, too, are summed up for the patient, so he can see as clearly as possible how the analysis is proceeding.

3. *Non-directive therapy* is a relatively recent development, the leading exponent of which is Carl R. Rogers. ("Client-centered Therapy," by C. R. Rogers, Houghton, Mifflin Co., Boston, 1951). He feels that the client can best arrive at a realization of what is wrong with him — and then of what he should do about it — if he is allowed to proceed in his own way, under his own power as it were and at his own pace. And so the therapist makes it a point *not* to put any new ideas into the patient's head, but merely to *repeat,* in other words, what the patient has already said, so he'll be sure to grasp it clearly. This is a subtle, delicate type of therapy, requiring great skill to conduct successfully. It is based on the view that the usual patient has a self-concept

of himself as a failure, but that if he is given the opportunity to think out loud in a quiet, permissive, friendly atmosphere, the forces within him of mental health and truth will lead him out of his wilderness.

4. Another school of psychotherapy is known as *relational*. It maintains that the patient's social relations are responsible for his maladjustment — which is a pretty safe bet. But it goes further: the therapist tries to *assume the roles* of those others involved in the patient's life. Sometimes, too, *psychodrama* is used, a technique in which the therapist thinks up a social situation that appears critical for the patient, then has the latter *act out* the various roles in this little play.

5. *Group* psychotherapy treats half a dozen or more patients, suffering from similar difficulties, about three times a week, for an hour or two each time. The group aspect breaks the ice and makes it easier for the patients to talk about what bothers them and to compare notes. Also, much more material and many more suggestions are forthcoming, to aid both patients and therapist. The latter feeds in to the group-discussions various considerations which he has gathered from individual conferences which he also holds with the patients.

6. *Conditioned reflex* therapy, announced in a book of the same name by Andrew Salter (Creative Age Press, N.Y., 1949) is based on the work of the great Russian physiologist Ivan P. Pavlov, (1849-1936) and his compatriot V. M. Bekhterev (1857-1927); *rather* than on Freudian ideas, which indeed Salter roundly condemns.

"We have only one thing to learn from psychoanalysis, and that is what not to do." (p. 22).*

Salter writes that he is constantly, in his work as an analyst, curing neuroses without having to discover their original causes (usually in infancy or childhood). He says this is possible because the neurotic personality is basically a *generally* inhibited one. He is fearful, anxious, holds-in his reactions instead of expressing them. The solution is to train this person to be "excitatory." "Each person presents a different problem, but the purpose is always identical — to provide a free, outflowing personality in which true emotions are expressed in speech and action." (p. 96).

Salter's six rules to become excitatory, and thus not dammed up and neurotic, are to indulge copiously in "feeling-talk" (emotional small-talk) ; "facial talk" (use the face muscles) ; to contradict people and attack their views *whenever* one feels so inclined; to use the pronoun "I" often; to express hearty agreement when praised; and to improvise one's actions from day to day, so as to feel as much freedom as possible.

Salter's method is simply to build a healthy, liberating idea (positive reaction) directly on to a neurotic, cramping idea (negative reaction) whenever possible. A wrong, unconscious conditioned reflex becomes a right, con-

*Salter makes no reference to the following fact, (as noted in "Personality And Psychotherapy," by Dollard & Miller, p. 9, McGraw-Hill Book Co., Inc., 1950): "Early, brilliant work on the unification of the great traditions of Freud and Pavlov has been done by T. M. French, ("Interrelations between psychoanalysis and the experimental work of Pavlov," in Amer. J. Psychiat., 89:1165-1203," in 1933) and R. R. Sears, (Psychol. Bull., 33:229-274, in 1936).

scious reaction; then finally with practice a right, unconscious conditioned reflex. Thus when a man suffering from claustrophobia remembered he had been trapped in a pipe six feet in diameter, and a workman inside had grabbed him, (this patient happened to remember the start of his trouble), "He was also to tell himself that the pipe broke open when the man grabbed him," (p. 66). In this way, neurotic chains of ideas can be broken, and healthful chains of ideas put in their place. Also, we repeat, excitatory actions in general must be substituted for inhibitory ones.

Salter accords a high place to hypnosis. In the preface to his book he says, "The first two chapters have been rewritten and expanded from my book 'What Is Hypnosis,' and form the basis of all that follows." Although there is much that is paradoxical and needs thinking through in this recent volume, it has a great deal in it which confirms and strengthens self-suggestion and self-hypnosis.

7. The next type of psychotherapy we shall mention hardly constitutes a school, since it refers to explicit *medical* techniques, which could be used by any psychiatrist (who must be an M.D.) regardless of which previously mentioned method he might favor. Also, medical aids are usually, for best results, combined with other, purely psychological aids. We lack space to do more than mention these kinds of physical psychiatry, which include shock therapy, psychosurgery (such as

prefrontal lobotomies,sympathectomies,vaginotomies and thyroidectomies), and narcoanalysis.

Specialized techniques which may or may not use medical aids include those for the crippled and disabled, alcoholics, and psychosomatic illnesses. Further techniques are hypnoanalysis, art therapy, dynamic therapy, and differential treatments for borderline cases.

8. The eighth "school" has been called *integrated* therapy, because techniques from all the systems are used in varying combinations, depending on the individual case and its needs. Since there is no one theory which is universally effective, and since there is much knowledge of mental hygiene yet to be discovered, the integrative approach is only sensible. Leading exponents of this liberal point of view require seeing a problem from many different angles. They combine a physiological aid, namely carbon dioxide therapy, with other techniques as the case requires. The carbon dioxide inhalation which they administer relaxes the patient gently and makes easier the *rapport* between him and the therapist, plus the *catharsis* of material with the concurrent analysis.

In closing this chapter, the author feels that age-old, everyday *prayer* is one of the great therapeutic aids of all time. It is closely connected with mental hygiene and with auto-suggestion, as we are soon to see.

CHAPTER VI

Self-Help Through Self-Analysis

So far in this book we have tried to show the structure of the situation that faces us. We are very suggestible. Each of us has very complicated conscious and subconscious minds. From the latter, motivations well up and direct us, unbidden and unsuspected. And, in the last chapter, we have noted the various ways in which mental troubles are approached and handled.

Since our theme, self-hypnosis, is a highly specialized technique, we want clearly to see its place in this entire scheme of things. It is one kind of self-suggestion; if truly mastered, the most valuable kind. It originates in the conscious mind, but travels into the subconscious mind, where it achieves its notable effects. We have already seen that hidden motives travel in the opposite direction, from the subconscious to the conscious. But in self-hypnosis we reverse the direction deliberately.

Why do we do this? Because whatever originates in the conscious mind can be *controlled* before it is sent on its way. And why do we want motives to operate in the subconscious? Because they then work *automatically*. We get their beneficial results while our conscious mind is left free for other things. There is still another advantage. The subconscious is a source of great *power*. If we learn to tap it, we derive tremendous benefit, arriving at our goals sooner than we would otherwise.

But obviously the benefits of self-hypnosis will depend on what we tell our subconscious selves to do. These benefits therefore can scarcely be greater than our wisdom. And so, before we study the specific techniques, we must appreciate the importance of correct self-analysis. Mental health and mental hygiene are needed as a framework from which we can then suggest to ourselves the things we need most.

It is foolish to learn *any* technique of action unless one's goal is well thought out. Yes, we can create in ourselves new conditioned reflexes, but we should understand just what we want to do with them. We should have a very clear picture of this "ideal personality" that we are urged to create. Exactly what does it include, and what is it supposed to exclude? If we are vague on this, our program must needs be vague.

Likewise, we can learn self-hypnosis. But this will only be valuable when we use it within a known framework of our personality-needs. In other words, careful pre-thinking is required before any procedures are adopted. We don't set out on a journey without knowing our destination. Before we learn self-hypnosis we must know what character-values we want, and need most.

Self-analysis is itself a valuable habit, and it has been said one should spend a part of each day at it. To start off on, here are some questions we may ask ourselves.

1. What actually are my life goals? Many persons are astonished to realize that they do not have clearcut objectives. It is one of the "Great Divides" between people. Some know exactly what they want out of life, and are therefore likely to achieve it, whereas the others are more or less drifters who, naturally, will scarcely get what they do not clearly know they want.

2. To what extent have I already secured my goals? Happy is the man who can feel that he has won what he set out to win. Of course usually we set up new goals when old ones are secured. Thus it may look at any one time as though we had not gotten much of what we wanted. But we should think back and remember all the things we did want to do, and did succeed in doing. This is only fair to ourselves. We should see how successful we have been so far.

3. What is holding me back from full achievement of my goals? What precisely? It is an excellent idea to write these obstacles down and study them. There may be several. Do I have bad habits which act as a constant drag on accomplishment?

4. Are these frustrations, these road-blocks of mine environmental, interpersonal or characterial? These are the three main types of difficulties encountered in life. The environmental are due to one's place in the physical world, or to happenings in it. A man who likes and needs the stimulation of big city life will not be happy on a deserted farm or ranch, for example. Environment covers a lot. Even a tire blowout is an environmental

frustration. An interpersonal frustration is due to a clash or unideal situation in connection with another individual. This would include an unsympathetic boss, a spouse who wouldn't cooperate, etc. A characterial frustration is due to one's own personality. A man is pulled two ways. He doesn't know what he wants to do; or he does know but seems to lack the talents or will-power to go ahead and succeed.

Much light can be shed on our frustrations if we sit down and spend a little time classifying and labeling them.

5. Which of these frustrations threaten me most seriously? This is the next step, to weigh and compare the various obstacles. There is no use becoming excited or over-concerned about some of them. Each life is different, but all lives are apt to have some frustrations that must be born with stoically. It is well to recognize what these are. Spinoza, in his famous "Ethics," is concerned to point out this valuable lesson to us, that each of us is probably trying to change things he cannot change, and also, conversely, is not trying to alter things that are within his power and that, for his own good, should be altered.

6. How can I overcome or lessen the obstacles that do seriously threaten me? There are many so-called defense mechanisms which we call into play when frustrated. They divide into three main types. Each type can be used justifiably or unjustifiably, depending on circumstances. The first is a reaction of aggression.

When we are balked of our wish, we often act more aggressively than before. We may "take it out" unjustifiably on someone else, as in "displacement," or we may work harder than ever to achieve our purpose. The latter, generally speaking, is the wise, justifiable form of aggression.

The second kind of reaction is flight or withdrawal. This is the least admirable of the three ways. Yet it has its uses. For instance, we often *identify* ourselves with heroes and heroines of the motion pictures. In film-stories, they usually lead lives of achievement, of which we are deprived. So we temporarily and subconsciously identify ourselves with them. Another defensible type of withdrawal from the rigors and disappointments of life is *fantasy,* in which we imagine the triumphs we have not yet secured. Sometimes this occurs in night-dreams. But we also have fantasy day-dreams; and so long as we do not indulge too much in them, they relieve the strain. "Several investigators have called attention to a general inwardness in the personalities of tolerant people. There is interest in imaginative process, in fantasies, in theoretical reflections . . . " ("The Nature Of Prejudice," p. 437, by Gordon W. Allport, Addison-Wesley Pub. Co., Inc., 1954).

The third form of reaction is to compromise with our frustrations. It is the "half a loaf is better than none" attitude. Sometimes this is a wise attitude to take. And maybe we can get more than half a loaf out of it. Sometimes, too, we realize we had originally set our goal too high, as when a young man, just out of college and in his first newspaper job, sets out deliberately to write the Great American Novel. He should first learn how to write, and then how to write a novel. Of two young women, both of whom want to be concert pianists, one has the required talents, the other does not. The latter becomes a music teacher, and will be able to lead a happy, useful life, depending upon her attitude. Compromise can be sensible and wise. It is informative to check up on this. How many compromises have we already made with life, and do we not feel they were advisable?

7. Do I really know what I'm best fitted for? Have I ever taken a battery of vocational and personality tests, so I can get an adequate line on my real capabilities? Am I acting even now without sufficient information about myself?

8. Conversely, have I ever made a thorough study of the opportunities around me in my vocation? Do I see the surrounding employment picture clearly? Have I noted the possible chances for advancement in my chosen field? To this end, do I know the right steps to take?

9. Would I actually be happy if I did achieve vocational success? Or do I have further emotional and personal problems that upset me, and that have little or nothing to do with my work?

10. Do I have any regular program for achieving success and happiness? Or are my thoughts along this line

conspicuous by their absence? Do I think about self-improvement every day, at some regular time; or only on rare occasions, perhaps, when I read a book of this type?

The above gives an idea of how one can set about analyzing himself, plus some key questions. To them may be added another. Namely, how much do I do to create happiness for others? A lot, or very little? Many world religions say such activity is the most valuable of all types. What is the opinion of the reader on this? Were your most valuable experiences, come to think of it, those in which you created happiness for others?

A good habit of self-analysis, if coupled with a mastery of self-suggestion techniques, can be the highway to success. We must admit, though, that self-analysis is not advisable for everyone. Psychotics, for instance, would not even be aware they needed self-help or any psychotherapy at all. Others might be aware of a problem, but misinterpret it. A person suffering from conversion symptoms, let us say some allergy, or asthma, might attribute them to an organic cause and not realize they were psychological. Other persons might feel incapable of either analyzing themselves adequately or effecting any real changes in their habits. But there are left many persons indeed who can recognize a problem they have, analyze it and either solve it or so reeducate themselves that it ceases to make them miserable and to absorb their time and energy. To the extent that we succeed in self-analysis, our confidence greatly increases.

The benefits are many. Says Prof. Gordon W. Allport, one of the country's leading psychologists, "Knowledge of oneself, research shows, tends to be associated with tolerance for others. People who are self-aware, self-critical, are not given to the ponderous habit of passing blame to others for what is their own responsibility. They know their own capabilities and shortcomings.

"Various lines of evidence are available on this point. The California studies of tolerant and prejudiced groups report that the ego-ideal of tolerant people often calls for traits that they themselves lack; whereas prejudiced subjects paint as their ideal pretty much the sort of person they are now. Tolerant people, 'being more basically secure, it seems, can more easily afford to see a discrepancy between ego-ideal and actual reality.' They know themselves and are not satisfied with what they find. Their self-awareness reduces the temptation to project their shortcomings onto others." ("The Nature Of Prejudice," p. 436.)

But we must be forewarned of difficulties. Many apparently valid reasons arise to obstruct the process of self-analysis. One's mind wanders off to other matters. All distractions from the work of analysis are welcomed. This is due to the very same "resistance" that therapists encounter when they try to help a patient. The law of inertia operates in mental areas too. "Habits tend to remain habitual." We don't want to change ourselves. At least the "old" part of us doesn't. But it is possible to decrease greatly one's resistance. We should tell ourselves, "I'm going to like learning this new habit. It won't take long."

Of course if training occurs in childhood, as so much of it does, we get the benefit of character-formation without having to understand it. But then we lack self-knowledge; we are simply products of a particular culture, or way of life. Among similar studies, the anthropologists Margaret Mead and Gregory Bateson have shown how much can be done in conditioning children. They spent two years in studying the child-rearing methods of the Balinese in Asia. The Balinese dislike to eat in public and avoid it whenever possible. So they train their children to dislike eating by feeding them when lying helpless in a bath, on their backs, and stuffing food into their mouths despite their tears.

The Balinese also show what they call "awayness" when in a social situation that demands too much of them. They do this by turning their backs on the people involved — sometimes even going to sleep. They train their babies to build up this same "awayness" reaction by borrowing other babies and loving them, ignoring their own babies before the latter's very eyes. (These facts have been clearly pictured and explained in "Balinese Character: A Photographic Analysis," pub. by N.Y. Academy Of Science, N.Y., 1942). "As the twig is bent, the tree's inclined."

Every reader of this book is himself a product of such social learning. Though he has been trained differently from Balinese and other nationals, he is nevertheless a product of *the same learning factors*. These factors operate sometimes in the conscious mind, at other times in the subconscious mind. And as we shall soon see, it is by no means a matter of indifference which part is used.

What are these all-important factors used in learning? They are, the world over, four: namely, drive, response, cue and reinforcement.

1. Drive refers to the motive that starts any act we engage in. The drive can be either innate, or learned. If innate, it is sometimes called a "tissue need." Examples are the need for food (hunger); for water (thirst); the need for air (called, when felt, anoxia); for sleep; need to avoid extremes of temperature, over-fatigue; etc. A learned drive would be, for example, desire to win social approval, amass money, etc. There are many more learned drives than there are innate ones. But drive there must be, otherwise there is no motive power for a learning habit to be formed.

2. Response is the act, or sometimes just the thoughts, by which the subject reacts to a drive. If no response is available, we can see how difficult it is for learning to occur. Thus, for instance, we could not teach a baboon about relativity, because he is *not equipped* with any response-mechanisms to our words. Response has to do, then, with how we are able to act on drives; and with what we do about them. We may build on to our drives either correct or incorrect habits. A habit is just an ingrained response pattern.

3. Cue is the stimulus to action or thought, and is thus a sort of trigger which starts them off. A cue is a stimulus which usually tells us when and where to begin responding to a drive. A green traffic light is a cue to go ahead. The drive is the desire to arrive at our destination. The response is our ability to get there in our car.

4. Reinforcement means reward. It is what strengthens certain of our acts and weakens others. When an act pays off, the psychologist says it is reinforced, meaning that this gives us the tendency to repeat it. When an act brings more pain than pleasure, or no result, it is said to have negative reinforcement, and will tend to be dropped altogether. Giving candy to a child for doing a household duty is a reinforcement. So also is his mother's approval when he does it without candy. Rewards need not of course be concrete. They can be mental and spiritual approvals, real and imagined, from society and from God.

We benefit greatly when we think about our drives, responses, cues and reinforcements *in terms of our conscious and subconscious minds*. Hypnosis and self-hypnosis are deeply involved here. For example, what happens when we form habits? Take a man who is learning to box. At first he is painfully conscious of every move he makes. But as he learns how to avoid punishment by blocking and slipping a punch, and how to deal it out by getting his weight behind every blow, however short, and by hitting vulnerable spots, what is happening? *His subconscious is taking over more and more of the work necessary for success.* This is the big point of our entire book. He is ducking punches automatically, without having to think about it. He is jabbing and hooking automatically, when slight cues, that he doesn't even have to think about, tell him he is within range.

His conscious mind has learned a great many lessons, and has passed them on, as accomplished facts, to his subconscious. So, when he wins a bout against a less skilled opponent, we are not surprised to hear his trainer say simply, "Our boy *knew* more."

Typing is another excellent example of how learning passes *from* the conscious *to* the subconscious. And this always means that a *habit* has been formed. Learning occurs every day, not just during "school days." This is perhaps the greatest fact of our life.

Let us go more fully into just what is happening here, in the next two chapters. And let us see how we can use the facts of self-analysis and learning for our own advantage.

CHAPTER VII

What Is Hypnosis?

Hypnosis is an artificially induced state, usually resembling sleep but physiologically distinct from it; in which the subject's suggestibility and powers are so heightened that he can perform astonishing feats of abnormality. By "abnormality" we do not mean pathological, undesirable, unpleasant or negative things necessarily. They can just as well be positive and highly desirable. We noticed earlier that hypnotism at first was unfortunately associated with neurotic and hysteric elements. We shall say more about this to prove that hypnotism is a tremendous force, neither good nor bad in itself, but waiting to be used for good. Waiting for persons like the reader. It is already finding daily use among hundreds of dentists, doctors and therapists.

There is no doubt that hypnosis is a mysterious force. This means simply that its nature is not well understood. But electricity is in the same class as atomic energy. They yield tremendous benefits. These are *results* of the forces mentioned, the latter being the *causes*. Usually we get a quicker line on such a force by studying what it can do, its effects and results, than by trying to figure out what it is in itself. So let us study first the general effects of hypnotism, and then ask ourselves what sort of thing it must be for such results to be possible.

[94]

WHAT IS HYPNOSIS?

Suggestibility itself is a *general* characteristic of hypnotism, and should be mentioned first, as it underlies all the specific effects. It refers to the great ease with which action or belief is aroused in the hypnotic subject. The abnormal accomplishments referred to above, are however just the second half of the same process. First, that is, the subject suspends his own critical and sceptical thinking, and *believes* what his hypnotizer tells him; second, he *does* the things suggested. Not only does the patient then *want* to do certain things; but he *can*. The fact that he can, proves suggestibility to be more than a mere attitude. It is a power, a general power. The normal susceptibility that we usually possess is referred to as greatly *heightened* in the hypnotic state.

This power is such that it can increase or decrease a vital function of mind or body. It helps us to see what hypnotism must be, and to regard its marvels in terms of *"pairs."* Let us take one such example, namely, anaesthesia and hyperaesthesia.

Anaesthesia is total or partial loss of sensitivity. The hypnotist suggests that certain real sensations are to be abolished, and they are. "Legs and breasts may be amputated, children born, teeth extracted, in short the most painful experiences undergone, with no other anaesthetic than the hypnotizer's assurance that no pain will be felt. Similarly, morbid pains may be annihilated, neuralgias, toothaches, rheumatisms cured." (Principles Of Psychology," by Wm. James, vol. 2, p. 606). As this standard text was published in 1890, we see that the wonders of hypnotism are not new. They never really were. Without question, the hypnotic state explains much if not most of the miraculous lore of the ages — feats of the yogis, "magical" performances by pagan oracles, religious ecstasies, the tricks of shamans, dervishes and medicine men.

The applications of hypnotic anaesthesia are very numerous, being limited by the ingenuity of the hypnotizer. Hunger sensations have been abolished in patients, so that they wanted no nourishment for days. Hard as it is to believe, patients have been pierced with needles, and have permitted the flames of burning matches to play directly on their hands without sustaining pain or any sensation.

Indeed, the hypnotist often begins by invoking anaesthesia in his subject. "You are to hear only my voice, you are to see only me," he directs. The subject obeys, and has what is called a negative hallucination. This can be reversed: a subject may be made blind *to* just one person, and not to others in the room; or deaf to certain words, and not to others. These hallucinations often become *systematized;* that is, they are generalized. For example, if a man is supposed to be invisible to the subject, what the man takes from his pockets is also not seen; what he says may not be heard; he may not be felt; etc.

Since there is nothing organically wrong with any of the senses thus anaesthetized, the sense-messages must, in these cases, be *blocked off* somewhere between the outside of the body where the sense-organ begins, and that part of the brain where "consciousness" results. The sense-message came in, but it was not recognized. It is something like "cutting an acquaintance dead," or refusing to recognize a claim. This fact is proved by experiments such as the following. Make a red cross on a sheet of white paper. Hypnotize a person and tell him he is not to see the red cross. He will not see it. Then have him look fixedly at a dot on the paper near the cross, and ask him what he sees. He will report a "negative after-image" of a bluish-green cross, which shows that his visual apparatus is working normally. He would not have had the after-image unless he had "felt" the red cross, so to speak, even though it never reached his consciousness. ("Principles Of Psychology," vol. 2, p. 607, James.) Such experiments demonstrate our great power of suggestion, of being able to *stop* the physiological action of nerves and brain at various points in their course.

The second member of this first pair of strange opposites is hyperaesthesia, which is simply an unusually heightened degree of sensitivity. It is the exact opposite of anaesthesia; and, in hypnotism, just as common. The powers of sense, depending upon which one the hypnotist stimulates, can be stepped up so much that one almost has to see such a performance to believe it. Some have wondered whether more than the ordinary senses are not needed for an explanation. We think not.

Acuteness of hearing increases. The ticking of a watch inaudible at more than three feet distance in the waking state becomes audible at twenty feet in some hypnotics.

Visually, a subject can often see with the naked eye details for which unhypnotized persons require a microscope. Or he may be able to read the image of a page of print reflected in a person's cornea. One famous test for visual hyper-acuteness goes like this. The hypnotized subject is shown a number of blank, similar sheets of cardboard, on one of which he is told to perceive some picture. No such picture is there but, through the power of suggestion, the subject creates a visual hallucination. and sees the suggested picture on the card. The cards are then thoroughly shuffled by the hypnotist. But the subject can always find the same card on which he keeps seeing the hallucinated picture. It makes no difference if the card has been turned over, or placed upside down. It is not because a picture is really there, that the subject always recognizes the card. It is because, unknown to himself, his sense of sight has noticed certain slight peculiarities about the card, which are too small for waking observation to detect. This experiment can be done in other ways, for example with empty glasses. If many of them are placed in a row, and the subject is told to drink imaginary water from one to quench an imaginary thirst, he will always find and use the same glass for the same purpose, no matter how the glasses have been changed around when he was not looking.

The sense of smell can be made similarly acute, as when an envelope, card or handkerchief is smelled by one hypnotized, then placed among many similar objects, and mixed. The subject, solely by its odor, will detect the original object. Braid reports the scent of a rose being traced through the air from a distance of forty-five feet.

The senses of touch, weight, temperature, etc., are similarly sharpened. A coin, for example, can be picked out from a heap of twenty other identical coins, over and over again, because the subject was told at the outset that this particular one was heavier than the others, or lighter.

The far end of this hyperaesthesia scale is still more astonishing. Subjects, through suggestion, can readily be made to have hallucinations of all kinds. Every one of the senses obeys the hypnotist's order and conjures up whatever is asked. A subject will "see" Napoleon before him. Or he will believe he is lying on a pincushion, and will jump up in pain. Or he will drink whiskey and think it water; or drink water and become as if drunk on whiskey.

Delusions or false beliefs are always m i x e d in with these hallucinations, the latter being purely sensory. You can make a subject think he is burning, freezing, itching, wet, covered with mud, insects, etc. You can make him drink vinegar and think it champagne; smell ammonia and be sure it is perfume; pay court to a broomstick believing it to be a beautiful woman; jump away from a chair that he thinks is a lion; imagine he is hearing a full symphonic orchestra, etc., etc.

The second major pair of strange powers involves memory. The hypnotic phenomena here can be ranged on a scale extending from partial or total loss of memory, amnesia, to hypermnesia, in which the subject remembers the minutest details extending back to infancy. As for amnesia, the hypnotic states, in themselves, are usually dissociated in the subject's mind from his waking system of ideas, which he completely forgets for the time being. But aside from this, the subject can be told he is not to remember certain things when he awakes, and he obeys. The memory can be turned on and off, like a faucet.

In hypermnesia, I recently regressed a young woman in the following way, before a classroom of students. I hypnotized her, then had her write her name on the blackboard. I then asked her to remember herself as she had been ten years before, and to imagine she was ten years younger. I had her write her name down as she used to do it then. I regressed her another few years in the same way, and had her write her name again. Each time she did this, her writing became more scrawly and childish. Her motor actions themselves were actually as they had been in those earlier years. Then I awakened her, and had her look at the signatures. One of the surnames she had written was different from her present one, and she recognized the former as her maiden name. She figured back and verified the fact that this had been her name in the year that I had regressed her to. Subjects can be regressed, in memory, back to pre-school ages until, when they write their names, the scribbles become unintelligible. A photograph and explanation of this is to be found on p. 195 of "Psychology And Life," by Floyd L. Ruch, 4th ed., pub. by Scott, Foresman & Co., 1953. This is a textbook used in the University of California at Los Angeles as an introduction to modern psychology.

If intelligence tests are given to hypnotized persons who have been regressed to earlier age levels, they will pass the tests with the actual mentalities they had at those ages.

A third outstanding pair of hypnotic controls runs all the way from the voluntary or skeletal muscles of the body to its involuntary or autonomic processes. Effects on the voluntary muscles seem to be the most easily obtained of all. Subjects are told they cannot unclasp their hands, open their eyes, lower an arm, etc. The most striking effect here, the one favored in vaudeville acts, is to cause a cataleptic stiffening of the body muscles, especially those of the stomach. The subject's head and feet are then placed on two chairs, and a second and heavy person can stand on his stomach, between the chairs. I strongly suggest that you do not try this experiment.

The involuntary body processes include the heart beat, blood circulation, digestive processes, sneezing, winking, etc. These too can be controlled by hypnotic suggestion. Space forbids telling the many experiments which have proved this. One can not only *induce* blisters and rashes by suggestion, but cases are on official record where stubborn skin diseases were removed under hypnosis. Such facts have become commonplace knowledge. In a syndicated medical column, "Dr. Jordan Says," which appeared in the Los Angeles Mirror-News on the very day this is being written, August 15, 1955, an article on "Warts Yield to Variety of Strange Treatments," ends, "The most astonishing treatment of all, however, is the method of suggestion. How the mind can have an effect on a virus disease is a mystery . . . It has long been known that warts which have been present for many years can disappear suddenly and completely merely by suggestion."

Various changes in cell nutrition, then, may be produced by suggestion — another fact pointed out by William James over fifty years ago. Thus, the metabolic processes of the body, involving both needful tearing down and building up activities, can be dealt with therapeutically, through hypnosis.

Besides all the unusual behavior, both voluntary and involuntary, referred to above, there is post-hypnotic suggestion. Here the subject is told, when in hypnosis, to perform some act upon awaking — which he promptly does without remembering why. Usually, it is done in the interests of experimentation or explanation of the nature of hypnosis. Sometimes they occur years later. Often they are done at the precise minute desired. It is as though a person, unknown to himself, were a subconscious clock which marked unerringly the passage of time. People who "set themselves" to wake up at eight a.m., and do so, have used their subconscious minds in this way.

The post-hypnotic suggestion makes us see that there are, and must be, definite organic connections between the subconscious and the conscious minds. What this may indicate we shall soon see.

The states of hypnosis and sleep seem so similar that it is well to dwell on the comparison a moment. Both involve relaxation, decreased inhibition, and emergence of the subconscious. Hypnotists often tell their subjects to "sleep," but the two states are not the same. Yet a hypnotized person, if left to himself, will often fall sound asleep. Probably the hypnotic state is the narrow stage just between being awake and going to sleep, and the skillful operator is able to keep the subject suspended there. This is called the hypnagogic period; and the moments between sleep and waking up, the hypnopompic period.

The position and attitude of the person to be hypnotized are like those of sleep. He is usually in a darkened room, kept quiet, told to relax, etc. But the first stages of ordinary sleep are usually dissociated ones, whereas those of hypnosis are narrowed down to unusual concentration and attention. Also the brain waves change, when we go to sleep, in three stages, whereas the brain waves of subjects being hypnotized "do not change as they do in sleep but remain entirely as they are in normal waking adults." And "sleep and hypnosis are basically not the same or even very similar." ("Physiological Psychology," Morgan & Stellar, pps. 551-2).

There are other differences. In natural sleep, consciousness may so far as we know be lost completely; but in hypnotic sleep it is not. For though the subject on waking may not remember what occurred, he can recollect it the next time he is hypnotized. Hypnosis may be more purely mental than is sleep, which brings with it changes in the circulation and chemistry of the brain. Hypnosis does not usually change the pulse, respiration and other bodily functions; but sleep does. During hetero-hypnosis (all cases other than self-hypnosis) the subject remains in *rapport* or some sort of social relationship with the hypnotist. In sleep, on the contrary, the self is quite detached from other selves, and rests. In hypnosis, the attention is fixed, whereas in sleep, either there is none at all, or it is associated with dreaming.

The vast and colorful variety of effects in hypnotism helps us to form a theory accounting for it. Actually it seems easier and quicker to say what hypnosis cannot do, than what it can do. So numerous and interwoven are the nervous mechanisms and connections in the body, that a path could be made from any part to any other part. The path for such an incoming sense-message, or outgoing motor-order, might be circuitous rather than direct, but it exists, and a neurologist could trace it for us. Thus, although such a connection had never been formed before, *a few words* from a hypnotist could result in, say, the rigidity of a skeletal muscle in a subject, or in blood activity causing the removal of a rash. We need to imagine merely an intricate maze filled with pathways, most of which have never yet been used. We know some of them are used *habitually*. As soon as we reflect that many other paths are there too, waiting to be used, we see what hypnotism, characteristically, does.

We must fully appreciate that words are triggers. They are not just little black marks on paper, etc. They are trigger-meanings, constantly setting off nervous processes. Sometimes they result in completed circuits, as when someone says, "Get the car serviced," and we follow up the reception of those few sound waves with an entire course of action. Even if we do nothing but understand the meanings of the words, they have become, as it were, living things for us, and have actually got inside us. An understood, spoken word must not only reach a certain part of at least one of a person's two temporal lobes in his brain, where his sense of hearing winds up, but it must also continue to the association area nearby, where the meaning of the sound is somehow stored. And so, when words help to become processes, the latter may continue farther than usual into or along the nervous system. They may end up in some surprising hypnotic effect. We have all the equipment for these possible connections all the time. When we realize this, we see that hypnosis simply makes *more* and/or *newer* connections than ordinary action does. It makes excursions into those areas of our nervous systems which are usually the independent kingdoms of the subconscious.

Consciousness is, thus, only a part of our minds. It is too much with us, and has assumed an overweening importance. The "instrumentalist view of conscious mind" is that its use is mainly to solve problems. Remember our discussion of habit. What we have already solved tends to become habitual, and to be done unconsciously.

Note how our ordinary consciousness *divides up the attention* that we give to our sense organs. As we sit here, reading or writing, we are seeing a little, hearing a little, feeling a little, and so forth. Even more clearly, as we move around walking, let us say, we are doing a little of many things . . . but not any one thing very much. Hypnosis shuts off most operations and has us concentrate on one. It keeps us from scattering our forces. The results we can, thereby, achieve are miraculous.

To say this in another way, it is as if the conscious mind were but loosely attached to the subconscious at a number of points or joints. The conscious part attends to deliberate reasoning, centers for us the spot of clearest vision, wrestles with new problems, interprets incoming sense-messages, etc. The subconscious handles all the old jobs, the already solved problems, takes care of the breathing, winking, digesting, blood-pumping, etc. Toward doing things any other way we always feel a strong *resistance,* which the hypnotist has ways of decreasing. Our normal design for living, therefore, is not the only way the conscious and the subconscious minds can be related. The connections are loose and can be changed and rearranged, for better or for worse, by the subject himself, or by what happens to him in life, or by a hypnotist. A person who suffers from a phobia, a morbid fear of, say, knives, darkness, closed spaces, heights, diseases, blushing, train-travel, appearing in public, etc., has literally hypnotized himself. This is true in the sense that habit is a relatively permanent hypnosis. His body *does* affect him unfavorably whenever he is in these situations, phobic for him, but it is only because of negatively conditioned responses which have become habitual.

Let us talk now about beneficial consciously conditioned reflex patterns.

CHAPTER VIII

Self-Hypnosis and Its Application

Self-hypnosis is destined to become, we believe, one of the great dynamic forces of society. Every human could learn to use this power for his own betterment. To review the strange history of hypnosis will help convince us of this.

Paracelsus (1493-1541), a Swiss alchemist and mystic, announced that the stars and magnets gave off a subtle force which pervaded space and could influence men. Van Helmont (1577-1644) brought the matter down to earth. He "inaugurated the doctrine of animal magnetism by teaching that a magnetic fluid radiates from all men and may be guided by their wills to influence the minds and bodies of others." ("History Of Experimental Psychology," ibid, p. 116).

It was Anton Mesmer (1734-1815), a Viennese physician, who discovered how to produce various cures by stroking people's bodies with magnets. In Paris, he constructed an oak chest filled with some chemicals and bits of iron. He called it a *baquet,* and had people sit around it in a circle. Gone was the presumed influence of the far-away stars. The *baquet* was the supposed source of this "animal magnetism" power, which Mesmer could control and direct!

Mesmer, togged out as a magician, made various passes and cast piercing glances at his circle, some of whom went into what we now know as hypnotic trance. Tremendous interest was aroused. In 1784 a French royal commission, of which Benjamin Franklin was a member, reported that the box simply was not magnetic. The French government then offered Mesmer 20,000 francs to reveal the secret of his cures. He refused — because he didn't know himself!

The results of the Mesmer episode were twofold. First, a new, astounding power had appeared on the human scene. Second, Mesmer's "refusal" caused both him and his power to be branded as a fake. The medical world and the public denounced him. He died in 1815 in Switzerland.

The second period in the history of hypnosis occurred in England. John Elliotson (1791-1868) was a medical man of big ideas. He helped establish University College Hospital in connection with University College, London, thus founding the invaluable practice of attaching a hospital to a medical school. He was the first Englishman to adopt the use of the stethoscope. In 1837 he saw a demonstration of *"Mesmerism"* by Dupotet, and began mesmerizing patients in his hospital. The authorities forbade this, whereupon Elliotson resigned, but kept experimenting. In 1843 he founded the "Zoist," which he said was "a journal of cerebral physiology and mesmerism, and their applications to human welfare." In 1846 he delivered the Harvey oration, reminding his medical foes drily that Harvey's proof of the circulation of the blood was also at first called fraudulent.

By 1849 "mesmeric infirmaries" were operating in London and elsewhere. At Exeter, the chief surgeon announced he had mesmerized 1,200 patients and performed 200 painless operations.

Even in 1842, W. S. Ward had amputated a leg painlessly, with the patient in a mesmeric trance. The use of mesmerism for an anaesthetic seemed assured. But in 1844 an American dentist, Wells, applied nitrous oxide to extract a tooth of his painlessly. Another dentist, Morton, began using ether vapor in Boston in 1846. And chloroform, through Simpson, came into use in 1847. Once again, hypnosis lost out. Its application and effects are highly individual. Though powerful, they vary considerably from one person to another. "The reason we do not use hypnosis nowadays for anaesthesia is that the drugs are more reliable." (ibid., p. 122). Even though James Esdaile (1808-1859), in India, had performed 300 major operations in painless mesmeric trance, reducing mortality in elephantiasis from 40 to 5 per cent, drugs became universally preferred.

A third bad break for this amazing force, hypnotism, then occurred. In 1848 at their home in Hydesville, N.Y., the Fox sisters began their mysterious rappings, and spiritualism was born. The sisters claimed they were "mediums" communicating with the dead. Seances produced new mediums by the hundreds; and still do. Unfortunately their powers were compared with mesmerism. Didn't they both deal in trances? So mesmerism became identified with the trickery part of spiritualism, and suffered even more disrepute!

Still in the second stage of our history occurs James Braid (ca. 1795-1860), called the discoverer of hypnotism. Why? Because he described the mesmeric trance as a "nervous sleep," coined the term "neurypnology" for it, leading to the word we now use. But above all, because he placed the proper emphasis not on the practitioner, who simply releases the hypnotic powers, but on the subject, who has them within himself. No more stars and magnets; just "nervous sleep." Braid, a Manchester physician, had been sceptical at first. But he forced a pin under the fingernail of a hypnotized theatre subject, and found her insensitive to pain. Braid began experimenting; became convinced. He hypnotized members of his own family. At first he thought the trance depended upon "paralyzing the levator muscles of the eyelids," called the "fascination method." Then he saw that not visual fixation but fixation of *attention* is the key. He used the word mono-ideism to describe the hypnotic state, stressed the factor of suggestion, and shifted emphasis more and more from the physiological to the psychological aspect. Braid helped create the modern view of hypnotism.

In the chapter on suggestion we sketched the third stage of this history, which developed in France. We saw that Le Bon's "The Crowd" unfortunately linked hypnotism with abnormal psychology. A fourth bad break! Actually in hypnotism we are dealing with the psychology of motivation, called "dynamic psychology." Freud is the great figure here, and he was the pupil of Charcot, who taught that anyone who can be hypnotized must be of the hysterical type, therefore "abnormal." This was a mistake. The rival school of Nancy said hypnotizability depended only on suggestibility — a power everyone has, and which is neither abnormal nor neurotic. But this has taken a long time to prove. Meanwhile Freud, who became immensely influential, took another tangent entirely, leaving hypnosis and developing psycho-analysis under the dominant idea of the "libido."

We are today in the fourth stage of the history of hypnosis, when realization of its power is rapidly growing. In the paper every few days, we read about another of its triumphs. Hypnosis has still a long way to go; but it has come a long way. And it parallels the history of science itself. For man's first scientific interest was in that which was *farthest away* from him, the stars. And the last great science to develop in time, concerns that which is closest to him, namely himself, or psychology. This is precisely the story of hypnosis. Paracelsus thought the power came from the stars. Today we know this power comes from within oneself. This explains why the sincere hypnotist wishes to teach *self*-hypnosis, so that the individual can unlock these powers for good that are *within him*. Even if we have not yet used this power, we do not permanently need a hypnotist. For each of us is his own hypnotist, his own magician. He himself can rub the lamp, and create the startling effects.

It is vital that we appreciate this fact. The great Emile Coue asks, "What then is suggestion? It may be defined as 'the act of imposing an idea on the brain of another.' Does this action really exist? Properly speaking, no. Suggestion does not indeed exist by itself. It does not and cannot exist except on the *sine qua non* condition of transforming itself into *auto-suggestion* in the subject. Auto-suggestion may be defined as the implanting of an idea in oneself by oneself.

"You may make a suggestion to someone; if the unconscious of the latter does not accept the suggestion, if it has not, as it were, digested it, in order to transform it into *auto-suggestion,* it produces no result." ("Self Mastery Through Conscious Auto-suggestion," p. 14–15, pub. by George Allen & Unwin, Ltd., London, 1951).

Another leading analyst says, "Though the practitioner may secure brilliant or strange results by hetero-suggestion (hypnotist to subject), we find, whenever we probe the matter to the bottom, that he has done nothing more than liberate the subject's auto-suggestions. If however the practitioner does not give the subject the key to auto-suggestion, the latter will believe that the former's influence is the cause of everything, and the results will be apt to prove extremely fugitive." ("Suggestion And Auto-suggestion," p. 204, by Charles Baudouin, 12th ed., pub. by Allen & Unwin, London, Eng., 1954).

The *application* of self-hypnosis is our subject. Here is how it is applied. First, you use your imagination to create attitudes for you. Second, these attitudes work in your daily life to do two things. *a.* They intensify your *inner drives* toward success. *b.* They keep selecting parts of your environment which keep helping you toward success. That is the mechanism stated simply, so that we can see there is nothing unbelievable about it. Self-hypnosis is unusual, true; but in the way in which *un*common sense, rather than common sense, is unusual. This uncommon sense of today, and of this book, will be the common sense of tomorrow! Let us now say more about the above two points.

1. *Imagination.* The beginner in self-hypnosis is surprised to find that leading writers on it stress the imagination rather than the will. Says Coue, "above all, and this is an essential point, the *will must not be brought into play in practicing auto-suggestion.*" Results are "unsatisfactory when, in treating moral ailments, one strives to *re-educate* the will. It is the *training of the imagination* which is necessary." (ibid, p. 17; italics his). Baudouin helps to give us the reason for this: "The work of suggestion goes on *in the subconscious,* and has nothing to do with the *conscious* effort which presides over the will. We may say that suggestion is a form of will, but of *subconscious* will." (ibid, p. 190).

That is, self-hypnosis involves the subconscious. Any resort to the will brings in consciousness and so disrupts subconsciousness. But, there is another reason for preferring imagination. It is, that the latter is *prior* to the will, and provides fuel for it. We will what we have already imagined. We see a new car, we think of it many times in imagery, and only then do we begin to will its purchase. We say "I want a car like that." Thus, in the delicate work of self-hypnosis, to concentrate on the will would be to put the cart before the horse. It is imagery that sets the will in motion. It is like saying "Take care of today, (imagination), and tomorrow (the will) will take care of itself."

A bipolar process goes on in each of us. 1. The realistic pole is that which is determined by *external conditions*, being characterized by *perception* of real objects, by reasoning and by problem solving. 2. The imaginative pole is determined by our *inner needs*, and is characterized by imagery, many kinds of play, fantasy, dreams and wishful thinking. This is the realm where self-hypnosis can operate. As our thinking shifts toward this realm, our mental images become stronger and more numerous. They are very responsive to our needs. We can order them up, control them, use them. Since they are the raw material of self-hypnosis, we must cultivate the habit of so doing. One is amazed and gratified at the progress he can make in this habit. And *all* the senses can be used for this. "Because visual images are usually the strongest and most frequent, it is easy to overlook other kinds. Nevertheless, if attention is given to them, auditory, tactual, thermal, olfactory, kinaesthetic (from muscles, joints and tendons), gustatory, and other sensory images are readily reported." ("The Psychology Of Thinking," ibid, p. 198).

The strategy is first, for us to do a great deal of thinking about what we want out of life, and should want, along the lines of the chapter six questionnaire. Then we have a "pre-hypnotic talk" with ourselves, in place of a hypnotist giving us one. During this talk, we say to ourselves such things as, "I am relaxing completely now, because I am putting myself into the right mood for self-hypnosis. I have thought carefully about the exact values I want to build into my life, and I'm going to get them. I'm going to get them by forming conditioned reflex habits in my subconscious, and this process that I'm starting now is going to ensure my success." We elaborate on this talk, and naturally change it according to circumstances and developments.

Next, we deliberately form images about what we want to be, get, or do. This should be, to speak naively, a lot of fun. The power of imagining, when cultivated, yields the richest of results. First you must devote yourself to discovering what imagery is available for you. If it is an obviously simple thing, like a new car, it is easy. See yourself buying it, driving it, enjoying it with others. See it, touch it, hear it — in imagination. Use every type of sense-image you can. Create them deliberately.

And the same for a house, a motorboat, a business of your own. Your desires need not be for "material" things, however. One can wish to become a good piano player, a Phi Beta Kappa, etc. Nevertheless, all these make up the class of *specific* images.

The other class is that of *general* images. These require more ingenuity to form. But they can and should be both formed and refined. Whatever it is you want in general, "success" or "happiness," *see* it in large shining letters just ahead of you, in your "mind's eye." As you give it other imaginative symbols, such as hearing a voice spelling it out or saying it to you, make it more specific. "Success" means a business of your own, or a doctoral degree in chemistry, or whatever you really and actually want. Now substitute specific for general images, and you have made a concrete step forward. *Imagining* is the activity that starts the ball rolling. Surely it is easy to see that this pleasant activity is bound to create *attitudes for you*. And since you have already thought out which ones you want to build, you are on your way.

2. *Attitudes*. Our second point was as to why and how these attitudes now start to work for us. According to the ideo-motor theory, which has had a long and honorable career in psychology, these success-ideas are dynamic. It is as though they had little motors. We plant them in our subconscious. They go underground, like seeds. But like seeds and other underground agents, they are ex-"seed"-ingly active, and will win the day. If planted right, they form powerful success-habits.

We said they would do two things for us: intensify our inner drives, and select for us parts of our environment which, again, will help us toward success. As for the first point, Shakespeare wrote "Love grows by what it feeds on." And we say today, "Nothing succeeds like success." Both are true. As our success-ideas work on the outer environment for us, make headway, and bear fruit, they react favorably on our inner drives, strengthening them. Remember the four elements of learning — drive, response, cue and reinforcement (reward)? The reward of success reacts on the original drive, giving us confidence in our judgment and our choice of goals.

Now how do success-ideas select for us what we may call "success-parts" of our environment? Well, imagine five men looking at the same plot of ground. One is a farmer — and he is wondering what the soil can be made to produce. A second is an artist, who sees the colors and contours of the scene, and wants to paint it. The third is a realtor, who considers how the ground would subdivide, and what bulldozing and pipe-laying are necessary. The fourth is a city assessor who is "using" the land only to figure a basis for taxation. The fifth man remembers he played baseball on this same soil as a boy; and he is filled with tender and haunting memories.

What differences in the attitudes of these five! Each *selects* from the outer environment what his inner *attitude* directs him to. And each *gets* from this same outer environment what he wants to get!

In precisely the same way, when each of us looks at the difficult life-road ahead, he sees it in terms of his *life-attitudes*. Let us now use this imagination we have been talking about. Imagine two men, pilgrims and wayfarers, looking ahead at a long, tortuous, stony road, winding through many passes and rising gradually to a far distant summit. One man concentrates on the dark mountain shadows, the dangerous ravines, the dizzying heights, the distance of the goal and the depth of the sheer, deadly drops. And he says "I can't make it." With that attitude, even if he tries, his chances of success are slim. But he probably never even starts the trip.

The other man concentrates on the road itself, keeping his studious eye on it steadily as the narrow ribbon leads him slowly up, in imagination, to the summit. He avoids the scare-sights that the other man is focussing on, and finally brings his gaze back down and centers it on *the very next step ahead.* Here all is visible and clear before him. And this brings him the happy thought that, "Every next step of the way will show up just as clearly when I actually get to it." Probably it will. This man will start the trip, and eventually reach his goal. He is no fool because he knows there are risks but never tells himself as he takes the first step, "I may not succeed." He refuses to think about not succeeding. Instead, he deliberately starts the journey with all his capacities exerted toward reaching the summit.

One man is setting up failure-symbols while the other is setting up success symbols. Both types of symbols are there, such as the shadow and the sun, the depths and the heights, so failure and success are also scattered along everyone's road of life. It is clear, then, that the inner attitudes with which we face the road ahead, determine largely what we see on it and along it. If we look at the yawning gulf below the connecting plank, we fall off. If we look at the plank, we get across. The latter is the only course to success. Why not follow this course?

Many of us find it difficult to be cheerful. And we may wonder about the relationship between cheerfulness and reason. Perhaps we ask ourselves, "What if the road ahead has more obstacles, dangers and terrors than it has aids for me? What if I can *prove* there are more chances for me to fail than to succeed? Then why should I be irrational and keep going forward?"

The solid and satisfying answer is to remember this fact, that we are bipolar, both *perceiving* external conditions and *feeling* inner drives, needs and goals. Of course the person who concentrates on the dark ravines and the dark sides of the clouds starts out by attending to the failure-symbols. He is off balance even for the external part of his job. But the real answer is this: — *one does not decide the course of a general action on the basis of environment*. This would be ignoring the great inner strength that each of us has by nature. For success itself, we depend on our inner motives, our *drive*.

Self-hypnosis is therefore to be applied as follows:

1. "Soul-searching." Formation of goals, ideals. Refer to questionnaire on page 84.

2. A pre-hypnotic talk with oneself. Relaxation; getting into the mood.

3. Imagining. Here we use hypnosis proper; a stage that is capable of great development in each of us.

4. Action according to the post-hypnotic suggestions already formed.

About this fourth stage, two points are important. *First,* this stage goes on during everyday conscious life. Our most dynamic success-ideas, even though they come frequently into consciousness, work subconsciously for the most part.

Second, you *can* learn to do this invaluable feat, sometimes called "thinking your way to success," if you take the time for it. If you fail to use the technique successfully, then you have not given it a fair trial. Most of us fail by not trying. We must remember it takes time to form any habit. Think how many years it took to learn to read and write, how discouraged we often were, and yet how invaluable this knowledge is. Think how painfully we learned to swim, to ride a bicycle, to ice-skate, to roller-skate. When it comes to self-hypnosis, we forget these things and want success in an hour. We can indeed achieve it, but we must realize we are forming a new habit and it will take time. We should work every day at it. If we do, we shall without question see ourselves progress.

We must decide what we want, and then visualize this. We may want to stop smoking, stop drinking, start being cheerful, start feeling more energetic, start taking steps toward business, literary or domestic success. Whatever it is, *these things certainly can be done.* So whatever you want to do, start working on it in the way stated above. Anyone who has felt a big increase in his energy, for example, and sees it stay with him day after day — all from "talking to himself" — will be sold on self-hypnosis.

Let us see how we can achieve the self-hypnotic state.

CHAPTER IX

The Techniques of Achieving Self-Hypnosis

We are in accord that wonderful benefits can be derived from the judicious use of self-hypnosis. The problem confronting us at this time is how do we achieve this highly desirable state? There are many procedures that will assure you the acquisition of self-hypnosis. Some individuals will achieve it by any procedure and others only through a technique that is especially suited to their needs. The important point to keep in mind is that if you persevere you will finally acquire the conditioned reflex pattern which is the basis of self-hypnosis.

Some individuals will achieve self-hypnosis almost instantaneously and others will succeed in this only after many weeks or even months. The reasons for this difference will be discussed in detail a little later. Your author has hypnotized and conditioned people for self-hypnosis within a matter of a few minutes. He has also been perplexed because of the many sessions it was necessary to spend with certain subjects before getting them into hypnosis.

Once you have hypnotized a subject, you need only give him a post-hypnotic suggestion that he can put himself under with a certain phrase or keyword, or by counting to three. This then acts as the stimulus for the conditioned response which in this case happens to be the self-hypnotic state. It is similar to Pavlov's dog experiment. Every time the bell rang, the dog salivated involuntarily. There are many other examples of the conditioned response mechanism, but the above example will suffice for our purpose of explanation. Once the subject has been properly conditioned, he can always bring about this stimulus response cycle. He accomplishes this just as fast as he can repeat the key words. Simple enough, isn't it? It is, when the subject responds easily. But when he doesn't, that's when we can run into a stalemate. Let us examine this more closely.

Many individuals have asked, "What is the easiest and quickest way of achieving self-hypnosis?" The answer, of course, is to be hypnotized and then be given a post-hypnotic suggestion that you can put yourself under by repeating a key word or phrase.

Thereafter whenever you wish to hypnotize yourself, silently count to three or repeat the key phrase and you will again be in the hypnotic state. Once in this state, you will be able to consciously give yourself whatever constructive suggestions you desire. These suggestions will then implant themselves in your subconscious mind and will work in a positive manner for you.

You learn to *apply* the following situation to yourself. Once a subject has been hypnotized you can always re-hypnotize him as he has learned to respond to hypnosis. The conditioning pattern has been established. You need only know how to bring about this response again. This is similar to sitting down to typewrite or to play the piano after a long lapse of time. As you begin to type or play the piano your fingers seem to move in an involuntary manner to the keys and notes. The same is true with any musical instrument. The conditioned response pattern is never lost, so to speak. It is lodged in the subconscious. Once the subject has been hypnotized the conditioned reflex pattern is set into motion. The proper stimulus will then produce the response which in our case is self-hypnosis.

Hypnosis has been defined as a state of exaggerated or heightened suggestibility, either brought about by a hypnotist or self-induced. How do you determine if a subject is under hypnosis? By giving him a post-hypnotic suggestion to carry out and observing if he does it or by challenging him to open his eyes or move a limb before you say a certain word or give him a certain count.

The subject has closed his eyes and you want to know if he is under hypnosis. You might give him the following suggestions: "When I count to three you will try to open your eyes but will find that you will not be able to do so until I reach the count of five." You proceed to count to three. If the subject opens his eyes at the count of three, you know the subject is not under hypnosis. If he tries to open his eyes but cannot then you know he is under hypnosis. Should you wish to determine the depth of hypnosis you can proceed to tell him that he cannot move an arm or foot until you give the predetermined count. Methods for deepening the hypnotic state and tests for determining whether the subject is in the lethargic, cataleptic or somnambulistic state are outlined in my two books, "Hypnotism Revealed" and "Advanced Techniques of Hypnosis." If you are not familiar with the technical procedures, you should read them. Should you want to determine if you are under hypnosis or the depth of the hypnotic state achieved, you would give yourself these same tests. You need only a light state of hypnosis to achieve beneficial results.

We know that the hypnotic state is characterized by extreme responsiveness to suggestion. You can use this information for conditioning yourself in self-hypnosis. Here is a standard procedure that you can follow. Lie down on a comfortable couch or sit in a comfortable easy chair. Choose a spot on the ceiling and keep looking at it. Now mentally give yourself suggestions that your eyes are becoming heavy and tired. Give yourself the suggestions that as you count to ten your eyes will become very heavy and watery and that you will find it impossible to keep your eyelids open by the time you reach ten. If you find that you cannot keep them open and have to close them, then you are probably under hypnosis. At this point deepen the state by again slowly counting to ten. Between each count mentally give yourself suggestions that you are falling into a deep hypnotic state. Give yourself suggestions of relaxation. Try to reach a state where you feel you are about to fall asleep. Some may get a very light feeling throughout the body; others may get a heavy feeling. Whatever it is, this is the time to test yourself to determine if you are under hypnosis.

If you respond properly to the tests, give yourself the post-hypnotic suggestion that you will be able to put yourself under later by counting to three, or using any specific phrase that you desire. You have achieved self-hypnosis and can benefit from it. Continue using it every day and give yourself the following post-hypnotic suggestion every time you work with it, that at each succeeding session you will fall into a deeper state and that the suggestions will work more forcefully with each repetition.

Let us assume that your eyes did not become heavy. *Then take a longer count.* You can count to one hundred if you need this period of time to assure an eye closure. The closing of the eyes is the first sign that you are in a receptive frame of mind. Let us assume that you get the eye closure, but other tests do not work. Take a longer count to get yourself in the very relaxed state. Once you achieve this, you should be able to respond properly.

Here are some instructions that must be followed each time that you work towards acquiring the self-hypnotic state. Regardless of the depth that you have achieved and whether or not you have responded to any of the tests, give yourself the following suggestions: "The next time I hypnotize myself, I shall fall into a deeper and sounder state." You should also give yourself whatever suggestions you desire as though you were in a very deep state of hypnosis. You may ask, "If I'm not under hypnosis, why give myself the suggestions?" You do this so that you will *begin* to form the conditioned reflex pattern. Keep at it. One of the times that you work at achieving self-hypnosis, the conditioned response will take hold - - - you will have self-hypnosis from that time on. It is like learning to drive an automobile with a clutch. At first, you must consciously go through the process of putting your foot on the clutch and shifting gears. Usually there is a grinding of the gears and you feel quite conspicuous about it, but gradually you learn to do this almost automatically and you gain confidence in your driving ability. The same is true of hypnosis. As you work at your task, you gradually get the feel of it and you achieve proficiency in it.

Are there any mechanical aids that will help a person acquire self-hypnosis? The answer is "Yes." We have at our disposal such aids as the hypnotic crystal ball, the hypno-timer, the metronome, musical records, hypnotic records and the hypno-disc. However, the use of these devices does not assure the success of hypnosis. They only *help* in establishing the conditioned response. Actually a spot on the ceiling is all that you need. Should you find that a particular device is suited to your personality, use it. More than once a person has told me that he didn't want to use the metronome as he was compelled to practice at a musical instrument as a child and this recalled unpleasant memories. Others respond favorably almost instantaneously to metronomes, etc.

We realize that the fascination technique is used to tire the eyes. It is our goal to take advantage of the conditioning process that has been established over many years of falling asleep when the eyes become heavy. When they begin to tire, it sets into motion the conditioned reflex pattern of falling asleep but instead of the subject falling sound asleep we actually purposely continue to talk to him and thus prevent him from doing so. In this manner, we lull the conscious mind while we reach into the subconscious. Many times if you stop talking to a hypnotized person he will fall asleep. Should you fall asleep while working with self-hypnosis it is perfectly all right as the suggestions will reach the subconscious while you are passing from consciousness to unconsciousness.

Since the tape recorder has become a household instrument, a novel yet effective way of inducing hypnosis is *now available*. It consists of the individual recording a hypnotic induction talk on tape and then playing it back to himself with the suggestions that he wants. Some people find it just too much effort even to give themselves suggestions once they have reached a state of quiescence. This solves the problem very nicely. I have had individuals achieve self-hypnosis in this manner when all other techniques have failed. With this procedure you can record a hypnotic talk for five minutes, ten minutes, an hour or whatever time you felt was necessary. (I personally feel that the length of time spent with the induction of hypnosis is not the criterion. In my practice, I find that most subjects respond at the beginning of the hour session rather than at the end of it. I rarely find that after continuously working with the subject for an hour does the subject finally succumb to hypnosis. It is a rather interesting observation.) The point therefore is, that you may record your own hypnotic talk, *however short*, and play it back to yourself. This might be *your* most effective device.

Of all the procedures that I know, I would say that the use of the hypnodisc and the hypnotic record are two of the most helpful and least expensive means of achieving self-hypnosis. As you probably know, the hypnodisc has the general appearance of a phonograph record. It measures twelve inches in diameter and has a hole in the center so that it can be placed on a phonograph turntable. As you watch this revolve it immediately tires the eyes and helps to put you in the proper frame of mind for hypnosis. It sells for one dollar and can be obtained directly from my office.

One of the main problems confronting most individuals is that they cannot avail themselves of professional help too readily in acquiring self-hypnosis. This is because there are relatively few men engaged in this work. This of course presents a problem. The most practical method of achieving self-hypnosis is to be hypnotized by an operator and given the post-hypnotic suggestion that you can put yourself under hypnosis by a key phrase. The advantages of working with a hypnotist are self-evident. No mechanical technique can take the place of this interpersonal help.

We are confronted with the problem of someone wanting self-hypnosis and not being easily accessible to outside assistance. I have already outlined techniques that you can use to assist you in achieving self-hypnosis. These procedures will work if followed diligently.

Since most homes contain a phonograph player, the use of hypnotic records has been instrumental in helping many to acquire self-hypnosis. It goes without saying that the conditioning process may take some time by this technique although many report achieving immediate results. The next problem is what type of a record should be made. What technique should be employed? What type of background should be used? It is evident that no record will be suited to everyone's needs and an attempt can only be made to make a hypnotic record that will have universal appeal with the hope that it will serve in instructing and conditioning those interested in acquiring self-hypnosis. I have experimented with many types of records containing various technical procedures and can tell you that it is impossible to devise a method that will please everyone.

You can, of course, make your own conditioning record to suit your needs. Should you have a tape recorder, you can experiment with various inductions until you achieve one that does the job for you. I repeat this because it is of the first importance for you to keep it in mind.

I have made two hypnotic records. These records have been instrumental in teaching the techniques of self-hypnosis as well as hetero-hypnosis. One record contains a musical background and the other a metronome background. I have had many comments on the records. I have had people tell me that the record helped them achieve self-hypnosis after the very first time that they played it and others tell me that it didn't work even though they played the record a hundred times. Why this paradoxical situation? Obviously the answer must lie within the individual himself. Perhaps the subject was really hypnotized but failed to recognize the hypnotic state. There can be many answers.

I have had cases where the musical hypnotic record worked after the individual had failed to achieve self-hypnosis with the aid of the metronome hypnotic record. I have had the converse of this situation as well. In the final analysis there is no set procedure that can be applied to every case. It is just a matter of trying each particular method. I have recently had very good success with a miniature hypnodisc about the size of a half dollar. This is covered with a transparent, finely grooved glass that refracts the lines of the miniature hypnodisc in a very striking and interesting manner. Perhaps the success of hypnosis in these cases is the result of this innovation. Perhaps this device was instrumental in finally capturing the full attention of the subject's conscious mind while the suggestions at last reached his subconscious. The point to keep in mind is that it is difficult to pin-point the success or failure of a particular method of induction.

I have made another hypnotic record dealing with self-hypnosis exclusively. In this record, the background of the music and metronome is left out. All that you hear is my voice. I have introduced some specialized techniques that I have found most effective in conditioning my subjects for self-hypnosis and which I hope will help you in attaining the art of self-hypnosis. Both sides of the record are concerned with self-hypnosis. The record is made of a 33⅓ RPM, break resistant construction and can be played on any standard phonograph player. It is titled, "Self-Hypnosis Record No. 3." It sells for five dollars and can be obtained directly from me. Write to : Melvin Powers, 12015 Sherman Road, No. Hollywood, California 91605.

As mentioned previously in this chapter, it is always best to avail yourself of professional help in attaining self-hypnosis. Over the last few years, numerous doctors have taken instruction in hypnosis. I would suggest asking your family physician to recommend someone to you. Your local hospital or mental hygiene society might also have this information.

CHAPTER X

If You Have Attempted to Achieve
Self-Hypnosis, But Failed

I should like to stress the following fact. The success of hypnosis does not depend so much upon the hypnotist but rather upon the subject. In the final analysis, the subject responds to hypnosis when he is ready both consciously and subconsciously to do so. We certainly realize that when an attempt is made to achieve the self-hypnotic state and the subject does not respond to it, the obvious explanation must be either conscious or subconscious resistance.

I have had many subjects tell me after they were hypnotized and conditioned for self-hypnosis that the reason I was not successful in hypnotizing them sooner was because they were not ready to "let go," so to speak. We must bear in mind that the hypnotic setting is an unfamiliar one to the subject and that naturally he feels a bit uneasy in this situation and is waiting for "something to happen." It is similar to that of going to a psychotherapist for help. The average person may find it rather difficult to relate himself to the therapist. He likes to feel his way in this interpersonal relationship and does not, as a rule, verbalize freely, until he is secure in this relationship. This identical situation is prevalent in working with hypnosis.

If the subject fails to respond to hypnosis, he may not be consciously aware of the reason or the area of resistance. It is the job of the hypnotist to overcome this resistance which at times can be very trying, to say the least. Of course, it is very gratifying for the operator when a subject responds easily to hypnosis and is conditioned just about instantaneously for self-hypnosis. The results, many times, seem miraculous. We are, as stated previously, primarily concerned in this chapter with those individuals who for some reason do not readily respond to hypnosis.

What is the answer to this problem? Obviously there is no set answer and one must use whatever techniques and methods he has at his disposal. You may be very well versed in the theory, technique and application of hypnosis but somehow you just do not respond to it. You may even state that you have no fear of hypnosis and have pursued this endeavor for some time. Let us see if we cannot throw some light on the problem.

The analogy, I believe, is similar to the patient with a neurosis seeking the help of a therapist. The former certainly wants to rid himself of the psychological disorder but the problem can persist even though the patient understands the psychodynamic mechanisms working in his case. It may take a long time to unshackle the symptoms of his maladjustment.

I would like to relate a common occurrence that takes place in my office. A subject comes to me stating that he would like to learn self-hypnosis. He tells me he has been working at it for a long time and has not been able to "get it," so to speak. Our conversation bears out the fact that the subject has hypnotized many individuals but he cannot put himself under hypnosis! Logically it would seem that this individual should understand the technique of acquiring self-hypnosis and have little difficulty in acquiring it. But this by no means unfailingly bears fruit. What is this seemingly insurmountable difficulty? Let us review the facts. The subject has no conscious fear of hypnosis, he has an excellent understanding of hypnosis and has even hypnotized and conditioned others for self-hypnosis but has been unable to acquire this state himself. I want to assure you that this dilemma, like all problems can be solved.

After we have discussed the subject's inability to achieve hypnosis, I decide to work with the subject and see just how far he does respond. An amazing thing sometimes happens! He responds immediately. The eye test works, the arm test works, he responds to post-hypnotic suggestion as though he had been hypnotized many times. The truth of the matter is that he has been hypnotized many times but he has not been aware of it. Within a matter of minutes, he is putting himself under hypnosis. He has acquired the art of self-hypnosis. He is an excellent subject. He is perplexed but happy. Where can we find the clue for this seemingly unaccountable immediate response? This, of course, is our challenge. Let me give you some of my thinking on this matter.

For many years, before I would begin to hypnotize a subject, I would have him answer a complete questionnaire regarding his conception of various phases of hypnosis. It was a multiple choice type of a questionnaire and the subject needed only to check one or two of several possible answers. Nine out of ten prospective subjects felt they would not be aware of or remember what happened while under hypnosis. Eight out of ten felt that they could be made to reveal "secrets" or information about themselves and be made to do things contrary to their will. Eight out of ten felt that they would be submitting their "will" to the hypnotist and that the hypnotist would have complete control of them. The subject was asked to rate himself relative to what type of a subject he thought he would be. Choices given were: Excellent, good, average, poor, very difficult. I would like to point out an extremely interesting result of this inquiry. I never got a response of excellent or good. Very few gave an answer of average and most rated themselves as poor or very difficult. They were equally divided on the last two responses. The above questions were interspersed among fifty in all. I felt the stated answers to be most informative. Let us discuss them in sequence and see what light they can throw on the subject of self-hypnosis.

The average subject feels that he will be "knocked out" when he goes under hypnosis. Therefore, as long as he can hear you or surrounding noises the subject feels that he is not *actually "under."* We know this to be false however, since he must hear you in order to carry out suggestions. The subject, though, rarely thinks of this and should you ask him if he is hypnotized, he will invaribly say "no."

You then ask the subject who is actually hypnotized to tell you why he feels that he is not under hypnosis. He usually says that he can hear accompanying noises plus the fact that he can hear you talking to him. Remember he feels that he must be "knocked out." You do not convince him though that he is under hypnosis until you challenge him to open his eyelids before you give the key word to do so. He is very surprised to find out that he cannot open his eyes or do other things of his own volition if you tell him that he cannot do it. By these tests you naturally convince him that he is hypnotized. You further clarify his misconception about being "knocked out."

Even when the subject responds by entering the somnambulistic state, the deepest in hypnosis, he still hears you and is fully aware of what is going on. It is only when you give him a post-hypnotic suggestion not to recall anything, that he will later claim he has not been hypnotized. Or he may admit he has been hypnotized, but cannot remember what he said or did, or what you told him during this period. In conditioning a subject for self-hypnosis, I always suggest to the subject that he will be fully aware of what has transpired since there is no need to have it otherwise. In fact, you want to make certain that the subject does recall exactly what he has said and done. This will go a long way in helping him achieve greater depth in the hypnotic process and reach his goal quicker.

You will recall that we were trying to determine why our subject, who was a good hypnotist himself, had responded so rapidly to hypnosis in view of his protestation that he was a very recalcitrant subject. Have you reached a decision? If not, let me tell you how I analyzed this case. It is my feeling that this particular subject, like many others, had already achieved the self-hypnotic state but was not aware of it. It may be likened to digging for gold in a mine that really has it. You have actually dug the gold, but discard it because you are unable to recognize it, since the gold needs processing before it will glitter. The same is true of acquiring self-hypnosis. You have the self-hypnosis, you do not recognize it, you disregard it and wonder why you haven't achieved it. The analogy would be similar to your telling me there was no gold in the gold mine because you had dug for a long period and could not find it. In reality you had acquired the gold but failed to recognize its characteristics.

The question in your mind may be, "Why *doesn't* the subject recognize it?" I think that he is looking for "something to happen" but is not sure himself what this something is and is positive that he does not have the hypnosis because he is aware of what is happening. He is not "knocked out" so to speak and because of this he reasons he is therefore not under hypnosis. This is a common mistake and one that I feel explains why many supposedly very difficult subjects respond immediately upon working with them for but a minute or two. I am fully aware that there may be many other psychodynamic factors working because the subject has availed himself of a professional hypnotist but I fully believe that, in the last analysis, the subject was just not able to recognize the self-attained hypnotic state.

The obvious question is, "How *can* you recognize when you have the self-hypnotic state?" The easiest thing to do is to give yourself an eye test or arm test. If you respond properly then you know you are in the self-hypnotic state. You can also give yourself a post-hypnotic suggestion such as that a cigarette will taste bitter. If it does then you know that you were in the hypnotic state or are still in this state. *It is usually very difficult for the subject to feel that he is in the hypnotic state.* Why? Because he does not feel any appreciable difference from his normal waking state. Many subjects will get a drifting or floating feeling. I can best describe this state as similar to that of falling sound asleep. In the moments just before sleep you are half awake and half asleep. You know you will be sound asleep in a minute or two. If you want to resist sleep, you can. But if you do not, then you will fall sound asleep. We experience this every night. For additional information on this problem of recognizing the self-hypnotic state see the chapter, "The Techniques of Achieving Self-Hypnosis."

I stated previously that at times the attainment of self-hypnosis can be quite complex and defy all the theories that we have at our disposal. A physician who was using hypnosis with gratifying results was interested in achieving the self-hypnotic state for a personal problem. He had tried by himself and failed and had also failed with the help of an associate. He had written me and asked what the chances were of my hypnotizing him should he come to Los Angeles. I should tell you that he lived in Florida and certainly this was not exactly a convenient trip as I am in Los Angeles. I can assure you that I did not encourage him to come here as one cannot determine if this will take one visit, one week, one month or one year. I suggested that he continue working with his associate. Another month went by and he wrote again saying that nothing had happened.

He decided to spend his vacation in Southern California and therefore would be able to see me. This doctor who I had supposed would require a great deal of conditioning went under hypnosis within three minutes after I started working with him. I am discounting the usual pre-hypnosis discussion. He restated his endeavor along these lines in person but I did not go into a long theoretical discussion with him since I felt that this would not help in his case. I proceeded to work with him within a half hour of the time that I first met him. I was surprised when he responded immediately to hypnosis. He was not only surprised but amazed. I cannot tell you why he responded so easily. The doctor could not relate anything that would give us insight into his case. He just said he went under and that was about all! I have presented this case to show that we do not have all the answers to this problem of the induction of hypnosis. I could have failed.

I have had very similar cases where I have failed after many attempts and am still puzzled because of the negative results. I believe that a further discussion of some other related factors may help us. I say may help us because every so often, even with all of our knowledge, we are still unable to help a person who is desirous of self-hypnosis. The complexity of the problem is similar to the physician wondering why a patient has an adverse reaction from a particular medicine, in view of the fact that the former has often administered this medication successfully. Saying that the patient has a sensitivity to the medicine does not really solve the problem. Essentially this is our problem with hypnosis. We can postulate many theories and point out cases where they would bear fruit admirably. But then we are confronted with the case where the subject should respond but doesn't. We are also presented with situations where we feel the subject will not respond easily — and lo and behold he responds immediately!

Let us examine the other obvious areas of resistance. Because most subjects feel they will be "knocked out," they also feel that during this time they will reveal things about themselves that they do not wish known. I suppose they acquire this idea from the movies and television plays. Invariably you will see a subject hypnotized and relating things about himself. Upon being awakened from the hypnotized state, he remembers nothing that he has said. You might say, "I have nothing to hide." I am not inferring that you do, but when the subject is confronted by this unfamiliar task, he many times begins to think that he doesn't want the hypnotist to know his innermost thoughts and therefore he goes along with the hypnotic procedure, but still resists until he is sure of himself in this interpersonal relationship. It is like trying to fall asleep while keeping one eye open so that you don't miss anything.

The hypnotized subject never begins to talk unless he is asked to do so. Should the hypnotist question him about a matter that the subject did not want to discuss, the subject would tell the hypnotist this. If the hypnotist persisted in this line of questioning the subject would wake up. May I call your attention again to the fact that the subject is always aware of what is going on. He is not an automaton who can talk and move only when told to do so by the hypnotist. Dr. Lewis Wolberg in his book, "Hypnoanalysis," (p. 176, pub. Grune & Stratton, 1945) states this very clearly and emphatically. This common misconception must be clarified before many subjects will allow themselves to be hypnotized.

Another stumbling block is the common feeling that

once hypnotized, the subject's will is easily subjugated to that of the hypnotist's. The subject feels that he will be subservient to every wish of the hypnotist. This attitude comes from the fact that in most fictional stories the hypnotist is always pictured as a "Svengali." He is never portrayed as an individual who has learned to use the power of suggestion for constructive purposes. And so we can see that when the subject decides to be hypnotized these conscious and subconscious fears can rise to create a mental block. You only have success in these cases after the subject is educated to the facts.

I should now like to discuss what I consider the most important problem to overcome if you are to achieve self-hypnosis. You will recall that I stated in response to a questionnaire which I had prospective subjects fill in, that just about all subjects rated themselves either as poor or difficult subjects. As long as this attitude persists, the subject responds neither to hetero-hypnosis nor self-hypnosis.

This common response held true for ninety-eight percent of the subjects questioned. The interesting and perplexing question is, "Why do subjects share this common view?" You might try to analyze your own feelings on this question. I see this problem in terms of a fractional equation. The strong desire to achieve self-hypnosis represents the numerator and the common denominator represents this negative feeling. Remember as with all problems this problem can be solved as well, if we know what to look for, and are given the proper key for the lock.

Perhaps the following information will help us in the solution of this problem. Ninety percent of the subjects questioned felt that a person with a "weak will" would respond very quickly to hypnosis. There seems to be a stigma attached to anyone with a "weak will." Should the subject thus respond easily to hypnosis, this would mean he has a "weak will"—which belief in the subject's mind doesn't carry a mark of distinction. It is looked upon as rather a debasing characteristic. Presumably, if the subject responds easily, he looks at himself as the "Mortimer Snerd" type of individual. Thus we once again see the inner conflict of wanting to respond and yet consciously or unconsciously resisting it. In most cases, I would say that these feelings operate on an unconscious level; yet they naturally affect the results.

I hope that I have given you some additional insight into the problem of achieving self-hypnosis. If you persevere you will finally achieve your goal. In closing this book, I would like to emphasize once again a very important factor. The success of self-hypnosis depends upon the receptiveness of the subject. In the final analysis, the subject responds when he is wholeheartedly ready to do so.

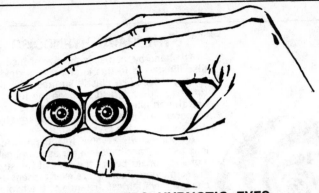

THE POWERS HYPNOTIC EYES

Here is an original technique that can be used very successfully in inducing hypnosis. The technique consists of using two glass eyes with eyelashes that close as you rotate the mechanism that holds the eyes in place. This action is similar to closing your eyes when falling asleep. You suggest to the subject as you hold these two eyes between your thumb and first finger that his eyes will become extremely heavy and tired as the eyes that you are holding begin to close. You then gradually begin to rotate your hand which causes the eyes to partially close. The subject, finding it extremely difficult to look at the eyes, begins to close his own eyes in unison with those that you are holding. You continue giving suggestions of hypnosis and before you know it the subject is under hypnosis. The eyes are the size of human eyes and are colored blue with brown eyelashes in order to give the exact effect of looking into real eyes.

The advantage comes in the fact that the subject begins to blink his eyes immediately and you suggest to him that this is the beginning of the hypnosis. It is just about impossible to look into anyone's eyes without blinking and this technique accomplishes this purpose. Using this knowledge, you incorporate it into your technique and induce the deep hypnosis accordingly. You can, of course, use this technique for self-hypnosis as well.

The Powers Hypnotic Eyes (1 pair) . . . $2.00

HYPNOTIC CRYSTAL BALL & CHAIN

I have had many request for a hypnotic ball and chain. I finally have been able to secure these and am offering them now for the first time. The crystal ball measures one inch in diameter and is actually made of genuine methacrylate which is crystal clear. A ten inch chain is secured to the crystal ball. You use this device the same as the regular crystal ball but this time you incorporate the pendulum effect which naturally causes the quick tiring of the eyes.

Professional Size—Hypnotic Crystal Ball & Chain . . . $2.00

THE HAND HYPNODISC

The hand hypnodisc is the size of the hypnodisc illustrated in this circular. It is rigid with a special lens-like plastic surface. The miniature hypnodisc is held between the first finger and thumb like the crystal ball and is used incorporating the techniques of the large hypnodisc as well as the crystal ball.

As you slowly revolve this hypnodisc, the lens-like surface causes a series of optical illusions to appear before the eyes of the subject. These moving illusions are ever present as you change the slightest distance of the hypnodisc from the subject.

This remarkable effect is achieved by the use of countless plastic linear lenses which separate the multiple images laminated behind them, permitting a different picture to change continuously as you change the angle of view or distance. Naturally this device is extremely helpful in capturing the full attention of the conscious mind of the subject and helps you to achieve the hypnotic state in the shortest possible time.

POWERS HYPNOTIC CRYSTAL BALL

The Powers hypnotic crystal ball is extremely useful as an aid in inducing the hypnotic state. It is desirable to use it as an object of concentration for your subject while he is being hypnotized.

The crystal ball lends an air of "mysticism" to the attainment of the hypnotic sleep and for some of your subjects this is the best approach in obtaining hypnotic control. There are individuals who will not react to a strict scientific approach to hypnosis and it is with these subjects that the use of such a device as the crystal ball is of inestimable value.

The crystal ball is held between your thumb and first finger, about twelve inches from the subject's eyes and slightly above eye level. The hypnotic crystal ball can easily be carried with you at all times.

As you know, the employment of a crystal to induce the hypnotic sleep is one of the oldest methods used in hypnosis. I personally favor this device and my students as well as myself have always had excellent results using this technique.

THE POWERS HYPNODISC
Copyright 1951 by Melvin Powers

An effective yet inexpensive method of inducing hypnosis is with the aid of the hypnodisc spiral. In my book, "Hypnotism Revealed," a picture of the hypnodisc unit with the hypnodisc spiral attached is shown. Above is a picture of my latest hypnodisc spiral. I am now offering the hypnodisc spiral as a separate unit which can be used with your phonograph turntable.

The spinning spiral will cause a series of optical illusions, causing immediate eye strain and fatigue. The subject feels that he is being drawn into a deep, dark revolving cone. By your suggestions of hypnotic sleep, you can place your subject in the somnambulistic state very easily. With some subjects, hypnosis will take place almost instantaneously. This technique is often employed in stage hypnotism.

The use of the hypnodisc spiral is also an excellent method of achieving self-hypnosis. As you concentrate on the revolving hypnodisc spiral, you give yourself suggestions of hypnotic sleep. You will note the optical illusions as they occur and the pleasant, relaxing feeling that accompanies these illusions. Giving yourself further suggestions of hypnotic sleep, you find that you are easily able to attain the desired state of self-hypnosis. This method is one of the most successful and popular techniques yet known for achieving hetero-hypnosis and self-hypnosis. At the Wilshire School of Hypnotism, all students in the self-hypnosis class are conditioned with the aid of the hypnodisc spiral.

During my lectures, I place the entire hypnodisc unit on the platform without having the spiral revolve. Continuing with the lecture, I note individuals in the audience gazing intently at the hypnodisc spiral. Invariably before the end of the lecture, many will have put themselves into a deep hypnotic state. This group self-hypnosis was achieved without my mentioning anything about the hypnodisc. These individuals assumed that the unit is used to induce hypnosis and their looking at it with that thought in mind produced the hypnotic state.

The hypnodisc spiral is printed on firm cardboard, measures twelve inches in diameter, and has a hole in the center so you can place it on your own phonograph turntable. It has the general appearance of a twelve-inch phonograph record. I am sure that you will be pleased with your purchase of the hypnodisc. The price is one dollar.

The hypnodisc is also available with four of the white spiraling areas colored in four different shades. The coloring is extremely interesting, fascinating, and very effective in inducing hypnosis as the hypnodisc revolves. The COLORED HYPNODISC sells for $3.00.

Send for POWERS HYPNODISC
Price . . . $2.00

CASSETTE TAPES

ONE HOUR HYPNOTIC RECORDS ON CASSETTE TAPE   **$10.00**

ONE HOUR HYPNOTIC RAIN RECORD ON CASSETTE TAPE   **5.00**

TWO HOURS OF MENTAL POWER RECORDS ON CASSETTE TAPE 10.00

ONE HOUR HYPNOTIC RAIN TAPE (3¾ IPS)

One of the chief assets of a good hypnotist is to be flexible in his approach in hypnotizing his subjects. As you know, it is necessary many times to adapt a technique that is suitable to the subject, and not to make the subject adapt himself to the method of induction.

We know that with somnambulistic subjects any procedure will put the subject under hypnosis immediately. The hypnotist gains complete control of his subject just as fast as he wants. Unfortunately, most subjects do not respond at the first session because of conscious or subconscious fears that must be gradually eliminated. Once you get the subject to relax, or "let go," he will naturally succumb to hypnosis. This is the problem that confronts all hypnotists.

Merely suggesting to the subject to relax or to "let go" is not sufficient, as a rule, to bring about this desired state. The subject, at this point, cannot turn on or off his mental and physical state of being this easily. Even if we have the subject lie down, this does not assure the hypnotic state, as the subject can still be tense. Our problem is how to get the subject to relax. Our situation is similar to the physician telling his patient to go home and forget about a certain problem. I'm sure that you'll agree that the advice is virtually impossible to follow

One of the major stumbling blocks in hypnotizing a subject, or in self-hypnosis, lies in the fact that although we use words such as: "relax," "let yourself go," and other similar terminology, the subject cannot readily put the meaning of these words into effect. It is difficult for most people to "let go" when we live in a society that beckons us to "look sharp," "be sharp," "be alert," "be on the ball" and "make every minute count." Emphasis on productivity does not lend to a society of relaxed individuals.

In my long experience as a professional hypnotist, I have tried many novel innovations for inducing hypnosis. Some have met with a great deal of success and others have failed. It is difficult to determine the causative factors for success or failure. We can only theorize.

I have used, over the last ten years, a technique that I shall describe now. Exceptionally good results have been attained with it; however, it is not infallible. It is suggested to you as another good technique. In order to help the subject relax, I have been using a one hour tape recorder recording containing the continuous sound of various degrees of rain. One half hour has a rain effect of very soft, light rainfall, as on grass, canvas or tent top. The other side contains a half hour of a rain effect such as one would hear in a heavy downfall with prominent patter of water on pavement.

The subject is instructed to close his eyes and listen to the sound of the rain while picturing himself relaxing near a warm, glowing fireplace. The relaxing effect thus produced enhances our chances for success in attaining a deep, hypnotic state.

The tape will play on all standard recorders and comes recorded at a speed of 3¾ IPS. The tape alone is worth $2.50. You therefore only pay $2.50 for the actual recording.   **ONE HOUR HYPNOTIC RAIN TAPE... $5**

A PERSONAL WORD FROM MELVIN POWERS
PUBLISHER, WILSHIRE BOOK COMPANY

Dear Friend:

My goal is to publish interesting, informative, and inspirational books. You can help me accomplish this by answering the following questions, either by phone or by mail. Or, if convenient for you, I would welcome the opportunity to visit with you in my office and hear your comments in person.

Did you enjoy reading this book? Why?

Would you enjoy reading another similar book?

What idea in the book impressed you the most?

If applicable to your situation, have you incorporated this idea in your daily life?

Is there a chapter that could serve as a theme for an entire book? Please explain.

If you have an idea for a book, I would welcome discussing it with you. If you already have one in progress, write or call me concerning possible publication. I can be reached at (213) 875-1711 or (213) 983-1105.

Sincerely yours,

MELVIN POWERS

12015 Sherman Road
North Hollywood, California 91605

MELVIN POWERS SELF-IMPROVEMENT LIBRARY

ASTROLOGY
_____ASTROLOGY: HOW TO CHART YOUR HOROSCOPE *Max Heindel* 3.00
_____ASTROLOGY: YOUR PERSONAL SUN-SIGN GUIDE *Beatrice Ryder* 3.00
_____ASTROLOGY FOR EVERYDAY LIVING *Janet Harris* 2.00
_____ASTROLOGY MADE EASY *Astarte* 3.00
_____ASTROLOGY MADE PRACTICAL *Alexandra Kayhle* 3.00
_____ASTROLOGY, ROMANCE, YOU AND THE STARS *Anthony Norvell* 4.00
_____MY WORLD OF ASTROLOGY *Sydney Omarr* 5.00
_____THOUGHT DIAL *Sydney Omarr* 4.00
_____WHAT THE STARS REVEAL ABOUT THE MEN IN YOUR LIFE *Thelma White* 3.00

BRIDGE
_____BRIDGE BIDDING MADE EASY *Edwin B. Kantar* 5.00
_____BRIDGE CONVENTIONS *Edwin B. Kantar* 5.00
_____BRIDGE HUMOR *Edwin B. Kantar* 3.00
_____COMPETITIVE BIDDING IN MODERN BRIDGE *Edgar Kaplan* 4.00
_____DEFENSIVE BRIDGE PLAY COMPLETE *Edwin B. Kantar* 10.00
_____HOW TO IMPROVE YOUR BRIDGE *Alfred Sheinwold* 3.00
_____IMPROVING YOUR BIDDING SKILLS *Edwin B. Kantar* 4.00
_____INTRODUCTION TO DEFENDER'S PLAY *Edwin B. Kantar* 3.00
_____SHORT CUT TO WINNING BRIDGE *Alfred Sheinwold* 3.00
_____TEST YOUR BRIDGE PLAY *Edwin B. Kantar* 3.00
_____WINNING DECLARER PLAY *Dorothy Hayden Truscott* 4.00

BUSINESS, STUDY & REFERENCE
_____CONVERSATION MADE EASY *Elliot Russell* 2.00
_____EXAM SECRET *Dennis B. Jackson* 3.00
_____FIX-IT BOOK *Arthur Symons* 2.00
_____HOW TO DEVELOP A BETTER SPEAKING VOICE *M. Hellier* 3.00
_____HOW TO MAKE A FORTUNE IN REAL ESTATE *Albert Winnikoff* 4.00
_____INCREASE YOUR LEARNING POWER *Geoffrey A. Dudley* 2.00
_____MAGIC OF NUMBERS *Robert Tocquet* 2.00
_____PRACTICAL GUIDE TO BETTER CONCENTRATION *Melvin Powers* 3.00
_____PRACTICAL GUIDE TO PUBLIC SPEAKING *Maurice Forley* 3.00
_____7 DAYS TO FASTER READING *William S. Schaill* 3.00
_____SONGWRITERS RHYMING DICTIONARY *Jane Shaw Whitfield* 5.00
_____SPELLING MADE EASY *Lester D. Basch & Dr. Milton Finkelstein* 2.00
_____STUDENT'S GUIDE TO BETTER GRADES *J. A. Rickard* 3.00
_____TEST YOURSELF—Find Your Hidden Talent *Jack Shafer* 3.00
_____YOUR WILL & WHAT TO DO ABOUT IT *Attorney Samuel G. Kling* 3.00

CALLIGRAPHY
_____ADVANCED CALLIGRAPHY *Katherine Jeffares* 7.00
_____CALLIGRAPHER'S REFERENCE BOOK *Anne Leptich & Jacque Evans* 6.00
_____CALLIGRAPHY—The Art of Beautiful Writing *Katherine Jeffares* 7.00
_____CALLIGRAPHY FOR FUN & PROFIT *Anne Leptich & Jacque Evans* 7.00
_____CALLIGRAPHY MADE EASY *Tina Serafini* 7.00

CHESS & CHECKERS
_____BEGINNER'S GUIDE TO WINNING CHESS *Fred Reinfeld* 3.00
_____BETTER CHESS—How to Play *Fred Reinfeld* 2.00
_____CHECKERS MADE EASY *Tom Wiswell* 2.00
_____CHESS IN TEN EASY LESSONS *Larry Evans* 3.00
_____CHESS MADE EASY *Milton L. Hanauer* 3.00
_____CHESS PROBLEMS FOR BEGINNERS *edited by Fred Reinfeld* 2.00
_____CHESS SECRETS REVEALED *Fred Reinfeld* 2.00
_____CHESS STRATEGY—An Expert's Guide *Fred Reinfeld* 2.00
_____CHESS TACTICS FOR BEGINNERS *edited by Fred Reinfeld* 3.00
_____CHESS THEORY & PRACTICE *Morry & Mitchell* 2.00
_____HOW TO WIN AT CHECKERS *Fred Reinfeld* 3.00
_____1001 BRILLIANT WAYS TO CHECKMATE *Fred Reinfeld* 3.00
_____1001 WINNING CHESS SACRIFICES & COMBINATIONS *Fred Reinfeld* 4.00
_____SOVIET CHESS *Edited by R. G. Wade* 3.00

COOKERY & HERBS

_____CULPEPER'S HERBAL REMEDIES *Dr. Nicholas Culpeper*	3.00
_____FAST GOURMET COOKBOOK *Poppy Cannon*	2.50
_____GINSENG The Myth & The Truth *Joseph P. Hou*	3.00
_____HEALING POWER OF HERBS *May Bethel*	3.00
_____HEALING POWER OF NATURAL FOODS *May Bethel*	3.00
_____HERB HANDBOOK *Dawn MacLeod*	3.00
_____HERBS FOR COOKING AND HEALING *Dr. Donald Law*	2.00
_____HERBS FOR HEALTH—How to Grow & Use Them *Louise Evans Doole*	3.00
_____HOME GARDEN COOKBOOK—Delicious Natural Food Recipes *Ken Kraft*	3.00
_____MEDICAL HERBALIST *edited by Dr. J. R. Yemm*	3.00
_____NATURAL FOOD COOKBOOK *Dr. Harry C. Bond*	3.00
_____NATURE'S MEDICINES *Richard Lucas*	3.00
_____VEGETABLE GARDENING FOR BEGINNERS *Hugh Wiberg*	2.00
_____VEGETABLES FOR TODAY'S GARDENS *R. Milton Carleton*	2.00
_____VEGETARIAN COOKERY *Janet Walker*	4.00
_____VEGETARIAN COOKING MADE EASY & DELECTABLE *Veronica Vezza*	3.00
_____VEGETARIAN DELIGHTS—A Happy Cookbook for Health *K. R. Mehta*	2.00
_____VEGETARIAN GOURMET COOKBOOK *Joyce McKinnel*	3.00

GAMBLING & POKER

_____ADVANCED POKER STRATEGY & WINNING PLAY *A. D. Livingston*	3.00
_____HOW NOT TO LOSE AT POKER *Jeffrey Lloyd Castle*	3.00
_____HOW TO WIN AT DICE GAMES *Skip Frey*	3.00
_____HOW TO WIN AT POKER *Terence Reese & Anthony T. Watkins*	3.00
_____SECRETS OF WINNING POKER *George S. Coffin*	3.00
_____WINNING AT CRAPS *Dr. Lloyd T. Commins*	3.00
_____WINNING AT GIN *Chester Wander & Cy Rice*	3.00
_____WINNING AT POKER—An Expert's Guide *John Archer*	3.00
_____WINNING AT 21—An Expert's Guide *John Archer*	4.00
_____WINNING POKER SYSTEMS *Norman Zadeh*	3.00

HEALTH

_____BEE POLLEN *Lynda Lyngheim & Jack Scagnetti*	3.00
_____DR. LINDNER'S SPECIAL WEIGHT CONTROL METHOD *P. G. Lindner, M.D.*	1.50
_____HELP YOURSELF TO BETTER SIGHT *Margaret Darst Corbett*	3.00
_____HOW TO IMPROVE YOUR VISION *Dr. Robert A. Kraskin*	3.00
_____HOW YOU CAN STOP SMOKING PERMANENTLY *Ernest Caldwell*	3.00
_____MIND OVER PLATTER *Peter G. Lindner, M.D.*	3.00
_____NATURE'S WAY TO NUTRITION & VIBRANT HEALTH *Robert J. Scrutton*	3.00
_____NEW CARBOHYDRATE DIET COUNTER *Patti Lopez-Pereira*	1.50
_____QUICK & EASY EXERCISES FOR FACIAL BEAUTY *Judy Smith-deal*	2.00
_____QUICK & EASY EXERCISES FOR FIGURE BEAUTY *Judy Smith-deal*	2.00
_____REFLEXOLOGY *Dr. Maybelle Segal*	3.00
_____REFLEXOLOGY FOR GOOD HEALTH *Anna Kaye & Don C. Matchan*	3.00
_____YOU CAN LEARN TO RELAX *Dr. Samuel Gutwirth*	3.00
_____YOUR ALLERGY—What To Do About It *Allan Knight, M.D.*	3.00

HOBBIES

_____BEACHCOMBING FOR BEGINNERS *Norman Hickin*	2.00
_____BLACKSTONE'S MODERN CARD TRICKS *Harry Blackstone*	3.00
_____BLACKSTONE'S SECRETS OF MAGIC *Harry Blackstone*	3.00
_____COIN COLLECTING FOR BEGINNERS *Burton Hobson & Fred Reinfeld*	3.00
_____ENTERTAINING WITH ESP *Tony 'Doc' Shiels*	2.00
_____400 FASCINATING MAGIC TRICKS YOU CAN DO *Howard Thurston*	3.00
_____HOW I TURN JUNK INTO FUN AND PROFIT *Sari*	3.00
_____HOW TO PLAY THE HARMONICA FOR FUN & PROFIT *Hal Leighton*	3.00
_____HOW TO WRITE A HIT SONG & SELL IT *Tommy Boyce*	7.00
_____JUGGLING MADE EASY *Rudolf Dittrich*	2.00
_____MAGIC MADE EASY *Byron Wels*	2.00
_____STAMP COLLECTING FOR BEGINNERS *Burton Hobson*	2.00

HORSE PLAYERS' WINNING GUIDES

_____BETTING HORSES TO WIN *Les Conklin*	3.00
_____ELIMINATE THE LOSERS *Bob McKnight*	3.00

____HOW TO PICK WINNING HORSES *Bob McKnight*	3.00
____HOW TO WIN AT THE RACES *Sam (The Genius) Lewin*	3.00
____HOW YOU CAN BEAT THE RACES *Jack Kavanagh*	3.00
____MAKING MONEY AT THE RACES *David Barr*	3.00
____PAYDAY AT THE RACES *Les Conklin*	3.00
____SMART HANDICAPPING MADE EASY *William Bauman*	3.00
____SUCCESS AT THE HARNESS RACES *Barry Meadow*	3.00
____WINNING AT THE HARNESS RACES—An Expert's Guide *Nick Cammarano*	3.00

HUMOR

____HOW TO BE A COMEDIAN FOR FUN & PROFIT *King & Laufer*	2.00
____HOW TO FLATTEN YOUR TUSH *Coach Marge Reardon*	2.00
____JOKE TELLER'S HANDBOOK *Bob Orben*	3.00
____JOKES FOR ALL OCCASIONS *Al Schock*	3.00
____2000 NEW LAUGHS FOR SPEAKERS *Bob Orben*	3.00
____2,500 JOKES TO START 'EM LAUGHING *Bob Orben*	3.00

HYPNOTISM

____ADVANCED TECHNIQUES OF HYPNOSIS *Melvin Powers*	2.00
____BRAINWASHING AND THE CULTS *Paul A. Verdier, Ph.D.*	3.00
____CHILDBIRTH WITH HYPNOSIS *William S. Kroger, M.D.*	3.00
____HOW TO SOLVE Your Sex Problems with Self-Hypnosis *Frank S. Caprio, M.D.*	3.00
____HOW TO STOP SMOKING THRU SELF-HYPNOSIS *Leslie M. LeCron*	3.00
____HOW TO USE AUTO-SUGGESTION EFFECTIVELY *John Duckworth*	3.00
____HOW YOU CAN BOWL BETTER USING SELF-HYPNOSIS *Jack Heise*	3.00
____HOW YOU CAN PLAY BETTER GOLF USING SELF-HYPNOSIS *Jack Heise*	3.00
____HYPNOSIS AND SELF-HYPNOSIS *Bernard Hollander, M.D.*	3.00
____HYPNOTISM *(Originally published in 1893) Carl Sextus*	5.00
____HYPNOTISM & PSYCHIC PHENOMENA *Simeon Edmunds*	4.00
____HYPNOTISM MADE EASY *Dr. Ralph Winn*	3.00
____HYPNOTISM MADE PRACTICAL *Louis Orton*	3.00
____HYPNOTISM REVEALED *Melvin Powers*	2.00
____HYPNOTISM TODAY *Leslie LeCron and Jean Bordeaux, Ph.D.*	5.00
____MODERN HYPNOSIS *Lesley Kuhn & Salvatore Russo, Ph.D.*	5.00
____NEW CONCEPTS OF HYPNOSIS *Bernard C. Gindes, M.D.*	5.00
____NEW SELF-HYPNOSIS *Paul Adams*	4.00
____POST-HYPNOTIC INSTRUCTIONS—Suggestions for Therapy *Arnold Furst*	3.00
____PRACTICAL GUIDE TO SELF-HYPNOSIS *Melvin Powers*	3.00
____PRACTICAL HYPNOTISM *Philip Magonet, M.D.*	3.00
____SECRETS OF HYPNOTISM *S. J. Van Pelt, M.D.*	3.00
____SELF-HYPNOSIS A Conditioned-Response Technique *Laurance Sparks*	5.00
____SELF-HYPNOSIS Its Theory, Technique & Application *Melvin Powers*	3.00
____THERAPY THROUGH HYPNOSIS *edited by Raphael H. Rhodes*	4.00

JUDAICA

____HOW TO LIVE A RICHER & FULLER LIFE *Rabbi Edgar F. Magnin*	2.00
____MODERN ISRAEL *Lily Edelman*	2.00
____SERVICE OF THE HEART *Evelyn Garfiel, Ph.D.*	4.00
____STORY OF ISRAEL IN COINS *Jean & Maurice Gould*	2.00
____STORY OF ISRAEL IN STAMPS *Maxim & Gabriel Shamir*	1.00

JUST FOR WOMEN

____COSMOPOLITAN'S GUIDE TO MARVELOUS MEN Fwd. by *Helen Gurley Brown*	3.00
____COSMOPOLITAN'S HANG-UP HANDBOOK Foreword by *Helen Gurley Brown*	4.00
____COSMOPOLITAN'S LOVE BOOK—A Guide to Ecstasy in Bed	4.00
____COSMOPOLITAN'S NEW ETIQUETTE GUIDE Fwd. by *Helen Gurley Brown*	4.00
____I AM A COMPLEAT WOMAN *Doris Hagopian & Karen O'Connor Sweeney*	3.00
____JUST FOR WOMEN—A Guide to the Female Body *Richard E. Sand, M.D.*	4.00
____NEW APPROACHES TO SEX IN MARRIAGE *John E. Eichenlaub, M.D.*	3.00
____SEXUALLY ADEQUATE FEMALE *Frank S. Caprio, M.D.*	3.00
____YOUR FIRST YEAR OF MARRIAGE *Dr. Tom McGinnis*	3.00

MARRIAGE, SEX & PARENTHOOD

____ABILITY TO LOVE *Dr. Allan Fromme*	5.00
____ENCYCLOPEDIA OF MODERN SEX & LOVE TECHNIQUES *Macandrew*	5.00
____GUIDE TO SUCCESSFUL MARRIAGE *Drs. Albert Ellis & Robert Harper*	4.00

HOW TO RAISE AN EMOTIONALLY HEALTHY, HAPPY CHILD *A. Ellis*	3.00
IMPOTENCE & FRIGIDITY *Edwin W. Hirsch, M.D.*	3.00
SEX WITHOUT GUILT *Albert Ellis, Ph.D.*	3.00
SEXUALLY ADEQUATE MALE *Frank S. Caprio, M.D.*	3.00

MELVIN POWERS' MAIL ORDER LIBRARY

HOW TO GET RICH IN MAIL ORDER *Melvin Powers*	10.00
HOW TO WRITE A GOOD ADVERTISEMENT *Victor O. Schwab*	15.00
WORLD WIDE MAIL ORDER SHOPPER'S GUIDE *Eugene V. Moller*	5.00

METAPHYSICS & OCCULT

BOOK OF TALISMANS, AMULETS & ZODIACAL GEMS *William Pavitt*	4.00
CONCENTRATION—A Guide to Mental Mastery *Mouni Sadhu*	3.00
CRITIQUES OF GOD *Edited by Peter Angeles*	7.00
DREAMS & OMENS REVEALED *Fred Gettings*	3.00
EXTRA-TERRESTRIAL INTELLIGENCE—The First Encounter	6.00
FORTUNE TELLING WITH CARDS *P. Foli*	3.00
HANDWRITING ANALYSIS MADE EASY *John Marley*	3.00
HANDWRITING TELLS *Nadya Olyanova*	5.00
HOW TO UNDERSTAND YOUR DREAMS *Geoffrey A. Dudley*	3.00
ILLUSTRATED YOGA *William Zorn*	3.00
IN DAYS OF GREAT PEACE *Mouni Sadhu*	3.00
KING SOLOMON'S TEMPLE IN THE MASONIC TRADITION *Alex Horne*	5.00
LSD—THE AGE OF MIND *Bernard Roseman*	2.00
MAGICIAN—His training and work *W. E. Butler*	3.00
MEDITATION *Mouni Sadhu*	5.00
MODERN NUMEROLOGY *Morris C. Goodman*	3.00
NUMEROLOGY—ITS FACTS AND SECRETS *Ariel Yvon Taylor*	3.00
NUMEROLOGY MADE EASY *W. Mykian*	3.00
PALMISTRY MADE EASY *Fred Gettings*	3.00
PALMISTRY MADE PRACTICAL *Elizabeth Daniels Squire*	3.00
PALMISTRY SECRETS REVEALED *Henry Frith*	3.00
PROPHECY IN OUR TIME *Martin Ebon*	2.50
PSYCHOLOGY OF HANDWRITING *Nadya Olyanova*	3.00
SUPERSTITION—Are you superstitious? *Eric Maple*	2.00
TAROT *Mouni Sadhu*	6.00
TAROT OF THE BOHEMIANS *Papus*	5.00
WAYS TO SELF-REALIZATION *Mouni Sadhu*	3.00
WHAT YOUR HANDWRITING REVEALS *Albert E. Hughes*	2.00
WITCHCRAFT, MAGIC & OCCULTISM—A Fascinating History *W. B. Crow*	5.00
WITCHCRAFT—THE SIXTH SENSE *Justine Glass*	4.00
WORLD OF PSYCHIC RESEARCH *Hereward Carrington*	2.00

SELF-HELP & INSPIRATIONAL

DAILY POWER FOR JOYFUL LIVING *Dr. Donald Curtis*	3.00
DYNAMIC THINKING *Melvin Powers*	2.00
EXUBERANCE—Your Guide to Happiness & Fulfillment *Dr. Paul Kurtz*	3.00
GREATEST POWER IN THE UNIVERSE *U. S. Andersen*	5.00
GROW RICH WHILE YOU SLEEP *Ben Sweetland*	3.00
GROWTH THROUGH REASON *Albert Ellis, Ph.D.*	4.00
GUIDE TO DEVELOPING YOUR POTENTIAL *Herbert A. Otto, Ph.D.*	3.00
GUIDE TO LIVING IN BALANCE *Frank S. Caprio, M.D.*	2.00
HELPING YOURSELF WITH APPLIED PSYCHOLOGY *R. Henderson*	2.00
HELPING YOURSELF WITH PSYCHIATRY *Frank S. Caprio, M.D.*	2.00
HOW TO ATTRACT GOOD LUCK *A. H. Z. Carr*	4.00
HOW TO CONTROL YOUR DESTINY *Norvell*	3.00
HOW TO DEVELOP A WINNING PERSONALITY *Martin Panzer*	3.00
HOW TO DEVELOP AN EXCEPTIONAL MEMORY *Young & Gibson*	4.00
HOW TO OVERCOME YOUR FEARS *M. P. Leahy, M.D.*	3.00
HOW YOU CAN HAVE CONFIDENCE AND POWER *Les Giblin*	3.00
HUMAN PROBLEMS & HOW TO SOLVE THEM *Dr. Donald Curtis*	3.00
I CAN *Ben Sweetland*	4.00
I WILL *Ben Sweetland*	3.00
LEFT-HANDED PEOPLE *Michael Barsley*	4.00

____MAGIC IN YOUR MIND *U. S. Andersen*	5.00
____MAGIC OF THINKING BIG *Dr. David J. Schwartz*	3.00
____MAGIC POWER OF YOUR MIND *Walter M. Germain*	4.00
____MENTAL POWER THROUGH SLEEP SUGGESTION *Melvin Powers*	3.00
____NEW GUIDE TO RATIONAL LIVING *Albert Ellis, Ph.D. & R. Harper, Ph.D.*	3.00
____OUR TROUBLED SELVES *Dr. Allan Fromme*	3.00
____PSYCHO-CYBERNETICS *Maxwell Maltz, M.D.*	2.00
____SCIENCE OF MIND IN DAILY LIVING *Dr. Donald Curtis*	3.00
____SECRET OF SECRETS *U. S. Andersen*	4.00
____SECRET POWER OF THE PYRAMIDS *U. S. Andersen*	5.00
____STUTTERING AND WHAT YOU CAN DO ABOUT IT *W. Johnson, Ph.D.*	2.50
____SUCCESS-CYBERNETICS *U. S. Andersen*	4.00
____10 DAYS TO A GREAT NEW LIFE *William E. Edwards*	3.00
____THINK AND GROW RICH *Napoleon Hill*	3.00
____THREE MAGIC WORDS *U. S. Andersen*	5.00
____TREASURY OF COMFORT *edited by Rabbi Sidney Greenberg*	5.00
____TREASURY OF THE ART OF LIVING *Sidney S. Greenberg*	5.00
____YOU ARE NOT THE TARGET *Laura Huxley*	4.00
____YOUR SUBCONSCIOUS POWER *Charles M. Simmons*	4.00
____YOUR THOUGHTS CAN CHANGE YOUR LIFE *Dr. Donald Curtis*	4.00

SPORTS

____BICYCLING FOR FUN AND GOOD HEALTH *Kenneth E. Luther*	2.00
____BILLIARDS—Pocket • Carom • Three Cushion *Clive Cottingham, Jr.*	3.00
____CAMPING-OUT 101 Ideas & Activities *Bruno Knobel*	2.00
____COMPLETE GUIDE TO FISHING *Vlad Evanoff*	2.00
____HOW TO IMPROVE YOUR RACQUETBALL *Lubarsky, Kaufman, & Scagnetti*	3.00
____HOW TO WIN AT POCKET BILLIARDS *Edward D. Knuchell*	4.00
____JOY OF WALKING *Jack Scagnetti*	3.00
____LEARNING & TEACHING SOCCER SKILLS *Eric Worthington*	3.00
____MOTORCYCLING FOR BEGINNERS *I. G. Edmonds*	3.00
____RACQUETBALL FOR WOMEN *Toni Hudson, Jack Scagnetti & Vince Rondone*	3.00
____RACQUETBALL MADE EASY *Steve Lubarsky, Rod Delson & Jack Scagnetti*	3.00
____SECRET OF BOWLING STRIKES *Dawson Taylor*	3.00
____SECRET OF PERFECT PUTTING *Horton Smith & Dawson Taylor*	3.00
____SOCCER—The game & how to play it *Gary Rosenthal*	3.00
____STARTING SOCCER *Edward F. Dolan, Jr.*	3.00
____TABLE TENNIS MADE EASY *Johnny Leach*	2.00

TENNIS LOVERS' LIBRARY

____BEGINNER'S GUIDE TO WINNING TENNIS *Helen Hull Jacobs*	2.00
____HOW TO BEAT BETTER TENNIS PLAYERS *Loring Fiske*	4.00
____HOW TO IMPROVE YOUR TENNIS—Style, Strategy & Analysis *C. Wilson*	2.00
____INSIDE TENNIS—Techniques of Winning *Jim Leighton*	3.00
____PLAY TENNIS WITH ROSEWALL *Ken Rosewall*	2.00
____PSYCH YOURSELF TO BETTER TENNIS *Dr. Walter A. Luszki*	2.00
____SUCCESSFUL TENNIS *Neale Fraser*	2.00
____TENNIS FOR BEGINNERS *Dr. H. A. Murray*	2.00
____TENNIS MADE EASY *Joel Brecheen*	2.00
____WEEKEND TENNIS—How to have fun & win at the same time *Bill Talbert*	3.00
____WINNING WITH PERCENTAGE TENNIS—Smart Strategy *Jack Lowe*	2.00

WILSHIRE PET LIBRARY

____DOG OBEDIENCE TRAINING *Gust Kessopulos*	4.00
____DOG TRAINING MADE EASY & FUN *John W. Kellogg*	3.00
____HOW TO BRING UP YOUR PET DOG *Kurt Unkelbach*	2.00
____HOW TO RAISE & TRAIN YOUR PUPPY *Jeff Griffen*	2.00
____PIGEONS: HOW TO RAISE & TRAIN THEM *William H. Allen, Jr.*	2.00

*The books listed above can be obtained from your book dealer or directly from
Melvin Powers. When ordering, please remit 50¢ per book postage & handling.
Send for our free illustrated catalog of self-improvement books.*

Melvin Powers
12015 Sherman Road, No. Hollywood, California 91605

WILSHIRE HORSE LOVERS' LIBRARY

____AMATEUR HORSE BREEDER *A. C. Leighton Hardman*	3.00
____AMERICAN QUARTER HORSE IN PICTURES *Margaret Cabell Self*	3.00
____APPALOOSA HORSE *Donna & Bill Richardson*	3.00
____ARABIAN HORSE *Reginald S. Summerhays*	2.00
____ART OF WESTERN RIDING *Suzanne Norton Jones*	3.00
____AT THE HORSE SHOW *Margaret Cabell Self*	3.00
____BACK-YARD FOAL *Peggy Jett Pittinger*	3.00
____BACK-YARD HORSE *Peggy Jett Pittinger*	3.00
____BASIC DRESSAGE *Jean Froissard*	2.00
____BEGINNER'S GUIDE TO HORSEBACK RIDING *Sheila Wall*	2.00
____BEGINNER'S GUIDE TO THE WESTERN HORSE *Natlee Kenoyer*	2.00
____BITS—THEIR HISTORY, USE AND MISUSE *Louis Taylor*	3.00
____BREAKING & TRAINING THE DRIVING HORSE *Doris Ganton*	3.00
____BREAKING YOUR HORSE'S BAD HABITS *W. Dayton Sumner*	3.00
____CAVALRY MANUAL OF HORSEMANSHIP *Gordon Wright*	3.00
____COMPLETE TRAINING OF HORSE AND RIDER *Colonel Alois Podhajsky*	4.00
____DISORDERS OF THE HORSE & WHAT TO DO ABOUT THEM *E. Hanauer*	3.00
____DOG TRAINING MADE EASY & FUN *John W. Kellogg*	3.00
____DRESSAGE—A Study of the Finer Points in Riding *Henry Wynmalen*	4.00
____DRIVING HORSES *Sallie Walrond*	3.00
____ENDURANCE RIDING *Ann Hyland*	2.00
____EQUITATION *Jean Froissard*	4.00
____FIRST AID FOR HORSES *Dr. Charles H. Denning, Jr.*	2.00
____FUN OF RAISING A COLT *Rubye & Frank Griffith*	3.00
____FUN ON HORSEBACK *Margaret Cabell Self*	4.00
____GYMKHANA GAMES *Natlee Kenoyer*	2.00
____HORSE DISEASES—Causes, Symptoms & Treatment *Dr. H. G. Belschner*	4.00
____HORSE OWNER'S CONCISE GUIDE *Elsie V. Hanauer*	2.00
____HORSE SELECTION & CARE FOR BEGINNERS *George H. Conn*	4.00
____HORSEBACK RIDING FOR BEGINNERS *Louis Taylor*	4.00
____HORSEBACK RIDING MADE EASY & FUN *Sue Henderson Coen*	4.00
____HORSES—Their Selection, Care & Handling *Margaret Cabell Self*	3.00
____HOW TO BUY A BETTER HORSE & SELL THE HORSE YOU OWN	3.00
____HOW TO ENJOY YOUR QUARTER HORSE *Williard H. Porter*	3.00
____HUNTER IN PICTURES *Margaret Cabell Self*	2.00
____ILLUSTRATED BOOK OF THE HORSE *S. Sidney* (8½" x 11")	10.00
____ILLUSTRATED HORSE MANAGEMENT—400 Illustrations *Dr. E. Mayhew*	6.00
____ILLUSTRATED HORSE TRAINING *Captain M. H. Hayes*	5.00
____ILLUSTRATED HORSEBACK RIDING FOR BEGINNERS *Jeanne Mellin*	3.00
____JUMPING—Learning & Teaching *Jean Froissard*	4.00
____KNOW ALL ABOUT HORSES *Harry Disston*	3.00
____LAME HORSE—Causes, Symptoms & Treatment *Dr. James R. Rooney*	4.00
____LAW & YOUR HORSE *Edward H. Greene*	5.00
____LIPIZZANERS & THE SPANISH RIDING SCHOOL *W. Reuter* (4¼" x 6")	2.50
____MANUAL OF HORSEMANSHIP *Harold Black*	5.00
____MOVIE HORSES—The Fascinating Techniques of Training *Anthony Amaral*	2.00
____POLICE HORSES *Judith Campbell*	2.00
____PRACTICAL GUIDE TO HORSESHOEING	3.00
____PRACTICAL GUIDE TO OWNING YOUR OWN HORSE *Steven D. Price*	3.00
____PRACTICAL HORSE PSYCHOLOGY *Moyra Williams*	4.00
____PROBLEM HORSES Guide for Curing Serious Behavior Habits *Summerhays*	3.00
____REINSMAN OF THE WEST—BRIDLES & BITS *Ed Connell*	4.00
____RESCHOOLING THE THOROUGHBRED *Peggy Jett Pittenger*	3.00
____RIDE WESTERN *Louis Taylor*	3.00
____SCHOOLING YOUR YOUNG HORSE *George Wheatley*	2.00
____STABLE MANAGEMENT FOR THE OWNER-GROOM *George Wheatley*	4.00
____STALLION MANAGEMENT—A Guide for Stud Owners *A. C. Hardman*	3.00
____TEACHING YOUR HORSE TO JUMP *W. J. Froud*	2.00
____TRAIL HORSES & TRAIL RIDING *Anne & Perry Westbrook*	2.00
____TRAINING YOUR HORSE TO SHOW *Neale Haley*	4.00
____TREATING COMMON DISEASES OF YOUR HORSE *Dr. George H. Conn*	3.00
____TREATING HORSE AILMENTS *G. W. Serth*	2.00
____WESTERN HORSEBACK RIDING *Glen Balch*	3.00
____YOU AND YOUR PONY *Pepper Mainwaring Healey* (8½" x 11")	6.00
____YOUR FIRST HORSE *George C. Saunders, M.D.*	3.00
____YOUR PONY BOOK *Hermann Wiederhold*	2.00
____YOUR WESTERN HORSE *Nelson C. Nye*	2.00

*The books listed above can be obtained from your book dealer or directly from
Melvin Powers. When ordering, please remit 50¢ per book postage & handling.
Send for our free illustrated catalog of self-improvement books.*

Melvin Powers

12015 Sherman Road, No. Hollywood, California 91605

NOTES

NOTES